FASHION
ART FOR THE
FASHION
INDUSTRY

FASHION ART FOR THE FASHION INDUSTRY

RITA GERSTEN

PROFESSOR FASHION DESIGN — ART
FASHION INSTITUTE OF TECHNOLOGY
NEW YORK

FAIRCHILD PUBLICATIONS NEW YORK

To my daughter, Louise and to my sons, Ben and
Kenneth.

Jacket and book design by Jaye Zimet

Copyright © 1989, Fairchild Publications
A Division of Capital Cities Media, Inc.

Standard Book Number: 87005-676-X

Library of Congress Catalog Card Number: 89:80056

Printed in the United States of America

CONTENTS

Preface   vii

ONE   **THE DESIGN SKETCH**   **1**
Research & Market Sketching   2
Fashion Forecast Services   5
Textile Houses & Fabric Information   8

TWO   **DESIGNERS & DESIGN PLANNING**   **11**
The Designer's Sketch   12
Design Exercise Using the Silhouette Shape   20
Free-lance Designer   26
Preliminary Presentations   28

THREE   **IN-HOUSE PRODUCTION**   **33**
Sample Sketch (or Workroom Sketch)   35
Workboard   40
Flats, Floats, Specs   46
Spec Drawings   52
Presentations   57
Recordkeeping Art   64

FOUR   **MERCHANDISING**   **69**
Showing the Line   70
Selling through the Sketch   75
Buying Services   78
Editorial & Showroom Art   80
Newspaper & Magazine Illustrations   84

FIVE   **THE SEQUENCE**   **95**

SIX   **RELATED AREAS**   **101**
Accessories   102
Patternbooks   104
Cosmetics & Fragrances   107

SEVEN   **YOUR PORTFOLIO**   **109**

AND IN CONCLUSION   115
ILLUSTRATION CREDITS   117

PREFACE

Where did that marvelous tennis outfit you admired on display in a store window come from? Or that stunning late day dress on the attractive brunette at a theater opening? Who put together that outrageous outfit worn to a rock concert? Is there a genius or deranged person in some studio dreaming it all up? Who is dictating long or short, baggy or fitted, colorful or muted, ruffled or tailored? How does it happen? So many garments, so much variety, season after season.

Using fashion art, *Fashion Art for the Fashion Industry* will take you through the world of fashion design . . . from the conception of the creative idea to the end result, the consumer's purchase. Numerous texts are available pertaining to fashion in the fashion industry: "how to" books on constructing garments, patternmaking, illustrations; books on textiles, advertising, marketing. You can find books on the history of fashion or on the famous and infamous personalities connected with it. This book, however, will attempt to explain the world of fashion from a new and different viewpoint.

Art is a major form of communication in fashion. In fact, it is inconceivable that fashion could function without it. If you are involved with the creation, production, education or business of fashion, this book will be of great assistance.

What goes into "climbing the ladder of success," or seeking a career in fashion? The three ingredients are creativity, training and last but not least, experience. Creativity is very difficult, if not impossible, to define. It is a special quality or ability, a gift called talent. How this unique quality develops depends on many factors including background, conditioning, confidence, acceptance and perseverance. Once creativity is recognized, training and experience should follow in order to reach successful and rewarding heights.

How many times have you said, "I used to draw or paint when I was younger", or "I'd like to have a job like yours"? Sometimes there is a bit of resentment in a person's voice when they say, "I thought of that, and now somebody else is cashing in on it". Without developing professional skills, without education and training, you cannot bring the creative idea to fruition. Training is the investment of time, energy and money in yourself and your future.

Experience takes time. Time to grow, time to try, and time to fail. Many of us do not give ourselves permission to fail. One must learn to adjust or perhaps compromise, and try a different road or method, change or go forward. When you succeed, and success will be yours if you persevere, the rewards and satisfaction will truly be earned.

In addition to learning drawing skills, the designer spends a greater proportion of time learning the technical skills of putting a garment together. Even though some of these skills will be performed by others in due time, it is essential that you, as a designer, have this knowledge to guide and evaluate others. The responsibility of the final results rests with the fashion designer.

Fashion Art for the Fashion Industry could not have been possible without the cooperation of designers, illustrators, manufacturers and publications. I wish to thank them all for their efforts and for permitting me to use their work. I regret that space did not permit me to include all the material submitted. I want to thank my colleagues at the Fashion Institute of Technology especially Walter Gerson, Community Resources; Phyllis Madan, Placement; John Corins and Maris Heller, Special Collections, Library. A special thank you to my students—whom I have taught and from whom I have learned—and whose work appears on these pages.

1989   Rita Gersten
                                              New York

FASHION
ART FOR THE
FASHION
INDUSTRY

ONE

THE DESIGN SKETCH

When you look at a beautiful garment, and think about how the idea came about, you first visualize the designer sketching at a drawing board. Ah, a genius! Some of us may think . . . I want to do that . . . others may say I can do that. I have ideas! Is it naive to think this way? No . . . not if you have talent, motivation, and can obtain the proper training and expertise. This unit has been planned to acquaint you with the first steps on "how" a design is created . . . the process and steps needed to begin designing. You will see how a creative idea is put to paper and the garment into production.

In this day of automation and high technology, the human factor is still the one ingredient in fashion that cannot be replaced. It is the individual creative talent that sorts out, accepts, rejects and interprets all the available information.

RESEARCH
& MARKET
SKETCHING

Fashion occurs in cycles. Yet it is never quite the same; there are always different interpretations, proportions and silhouettes. Technology and techniques are constantly advancing and changing.

No one will contest the fact that in fashion the past exerts a very strong influence on the present. One can "read" the story of people and their times by the clothes they wore. Where do designers find information on the past?

- ◆ Costume museums and special costume exhibits
- ◆ Books on the history of fashion, art, lifestyles, etc.
- ◆ Old issues of fashion magazines
- ◆ Fashion records
- ◆ Ancient artifacts

Creative individuals have finely tuned antennae. Instinct and a strong ego are just two of a creative designer's traits. You should be aware of cultural, political and social changes. These factors all affect the lifestyle of your customers and ultimately the clothes they will wear.

Every designer and manufacturer must keep abreast of the current situation in the apparel industry. What are the stores featuring in their windows? Where are specific garments displayed? What is moving? A designer and manufacturer must be aware of their line as well as their competitor's. Future planning and changes are affected by the knowledge gathered in the marketplace ... **Researching the market!**

Your equipment should be lightweight and easy to handle for any research trip. Work quickly in public viewing areas; do not attempt a finished sketch. Your first visual impression will have a special, refreshing charm. Be sure to make all notations pertinent to the assignment.

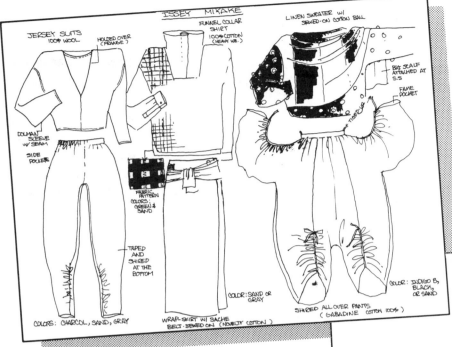

* DETAIL POCKETS WITH GLOVES

* JEAN-PAUL GAULTER'S SWEATERSHIRT AT "IF" IN SOHO

* ISSEY MIYAKE'S COTTON-QUILTED JACKET WITH FRINGES AT DIANNE B. IN SOHO

These examples represent a student's market research of clothing sold in the Soho neighborhood of New York. They are finished, and provide information to continue the design process.

FASHION FORECAST SERVICES

The fashion industry is complex and multi-faceted. It is impossible to attend all the fashion shows, conventions, seminars, openings, textile fairs, etc., and still have time to create, plan and execute a line. Hence, the growing industry of forecast services.

In the past, individuals attended the important European openings and serviced an elite clientele with sketches and reports. Today this is not sufficient. Many designers, manufacturers and buying houses rely heavily on forecast services for information. A good service can select new directions, trends and details. They research the market worldwide. Reports cover established and new designers. The accessory and other specialized markets are also covered. All this information is communicated through the fashion art sketch.

Some forecast services have facilities available for private consultations, slide showings and display.

a fashion view with a point-of-view

here & there

KEY BODY SHAPES

1. Short and Sweet.
   • Puffed sleevehead.
   • Elbow-length rib.
2. Abbreviated Cardigan.
   • Deep-scoop neckline.
   • Same-length sleeves and body.
3. The Bardot Top.
   • Portrait neckline.
   • Body-fit shaping.
4. Dolman Bolero.
   • Curvy cut.
   • Elbow length sleeves.
5. New-Couture Dolman.
   • Curved shoulderline.
   • Fitted cropped waist.

Nigel French

WOMENSWEAR
FORECAST
COLOUR FABRIC STYLING

SPRING SUMMER '88

Forecast services use a combination of figures and flats to get their message across to their clients. These pages from a Nigel French forecast manual include merchandising flats, silhouette and styling illustrations. The different types of art serve different purposes within the same group.

REPORT FROM TOBÉ

Report From London
A-E

One Enchanted Evening
G-K

American Gothic Spirit
1-13

Tiering Up
15-20

Naked Leat
67-71

The Italian S
81-93

ASSOCIATES INC.
OCTOBER 21, 1986

ELEMENTS OF STYLE

THE HIGH WAIST

Cotton viscose cropped turtleneck sweater, #59953, 55.00; wool crepe high-waist pants with back zipper, #50223, 67.50. ANNE KLEIN II.

Wool gabardine shawl-collar single-button jacket, #140018, 84.00; matching high-rise yoked pants, #140024, 48.00. TAHARI.

Linen blend plaid two pocket jacket with side elastic, #7308, 100.00; matching plaid high-waist slim skirt, #7115, 60.00. CALVIN KLEIN.

CONTENTS © TOBÉ ASSOCIATES, INC. 26

TOBÉ

Here, pages from a Tobé Associates catalog include a report on the designer, style number and wholesale price.

TEXTILE HOUSES & FABRIC INFORMATION

The textile industry covers a multitude of areas and processes ... from color laboratories to conversion of goods; from weaving to piece goods; natural fibers, synthetics, and a combination of both. Since our focus is on fashion art in the fashion industry, the main thrust of this unit as it relates to the design stage will be the direct relationship between the textile and fabric source and the designer or manufacturer.

The textile industry must get samples of available goods into the market early in the design process. Textile and fabric shows, sales reps, showrooms, advertising promotions are all used. At one time a textile manufacturer staged productions featuring star personalities that rivaled a Broadway musical to promote their new product.

Special promotional catalogues are widely used to reach the attention of the designer. They contain fashion drawings along with fabric swatches and color choices. The fashion art tends to show fashion direction as seen by a particular textile house and their product in the market. The figures are usually stylized and simplified. The art may also suggest ways to combine various textures, colors and patterns.

FLY-AWAY JACKETS flat fronts • swing backs • rounded shoulders • diverse lengths • shirting to suiting weight fabrics

shirt cuff

band neck

shawl collar

saddle raglan

patch pocket

rib cage length

suit cuff

hip bone length

wrist length

patch pockets

3/4 length

A

23

24

26

25

OH SO CLASSIC!

COLOR
• Golden browns
• Winter white and chalky pastels
• Gypsum
• "Regimental classic darks" — Claret, Lacquer, and Evergreen

FABRIC
• Gabardine/twills
• Cotton tweeds
• Whipcords
• Bedford cords
• Brushed and sueded cottons
• Flannels
• Heather knits
• Heavy-gauge sweater knits
• Jersey
• Corduroy
• Velvets with sateens

PRINT & PATTERN
• Houndstooth
• Small tattersall checks
• Blanket plaids
• Windowpane
• Regimental stripes

DESIGN
• Structured knit twin-sets
• Polo sweaters
• High or low mock turtlenecks
• Ankle-length pleated skirts
• Fit and flared/circular skirts
• Wider and relaxed cuffed slacks
• Straight and seamed skirts

Textile companies use a variety of formats to keep their clients abreast of what's happening in the world of fashion. Pages from a Cotton Incorporated catalog (center and bottom) include sketches and fabric swatches anticipating trends in women's and men's wear. Also included is a dramatic color photo of a section of a garment made in the "forecast" fabric. Celanese Corporation (top), on the other hand, uses sketches and simple, but informative, callouts.

TWO

DESIGNERS & DESIGN PLANNING

The role and the responsibilities of the designer before the garment is approved for production are discussed on the following pages. Examples of conceptual sketches, presentation drawings, and the many steps in between are included. The fashion art sketch is used extensively in this phase of the design process. The role of the free-lance designer is important to the fashion industry, and is also explored in this unit.

The work of many designers is included, some are better known than others. They are by no means representative of all categories, levels or types of the fashion industry. Space does not permit me to include as many as I would like.

THE DESIGNER'S SKETCH

The fashion designer communicates through a sketch ... the technique and style is purely individual and based on the designer's background, taste level, subconscious, perception. It is understood that the design will fit into the category and price range of the manufacturer. The basic information is received and absorbed through research, forecasting services, etc.

Some designers do not draw very well, others are capable of producing finished, detailed renderings. The important point to remember is the purpose or goal of the creative designer sketch—to communicate an idea or concept visually. The "designer" is thinking on paper. As the mind works faster than the hand, the idea can be shown with a few lines with changes, notations and crossouts. As long as the sketch transmits the proportion, the silhouette and details of the garment envisioned by the designer, it is a good and successful design sketch. If not, it doesn't matter how "good" the drawing ability of the designer.

Designers "create" in different ways depending on their skills and training as artists, time and pressure, the procedures used in a particular firm, and the area of design, for example, sportswear or evening wear.

Many designers leave the finishing of the sketch to their assistants. Others may take their design sketch into a workroom or to the sample stage.

Designer Michael Kors uses his company's pads to sketch his design ideas. The entire look is completed in color with fabric swatches and memos giving specific instructions.

The whimsy and fun of Betsey Johnson's sketches reflect her designs and personality. On the other hand, the designs by Louis Dell'Olio (facing page) reflect the ultimate in sophistication.

The charm of the late Willi Smith's designs is evident in these sketches by the designer.

Willi Smith
Spring 1987

Willi Smith 87

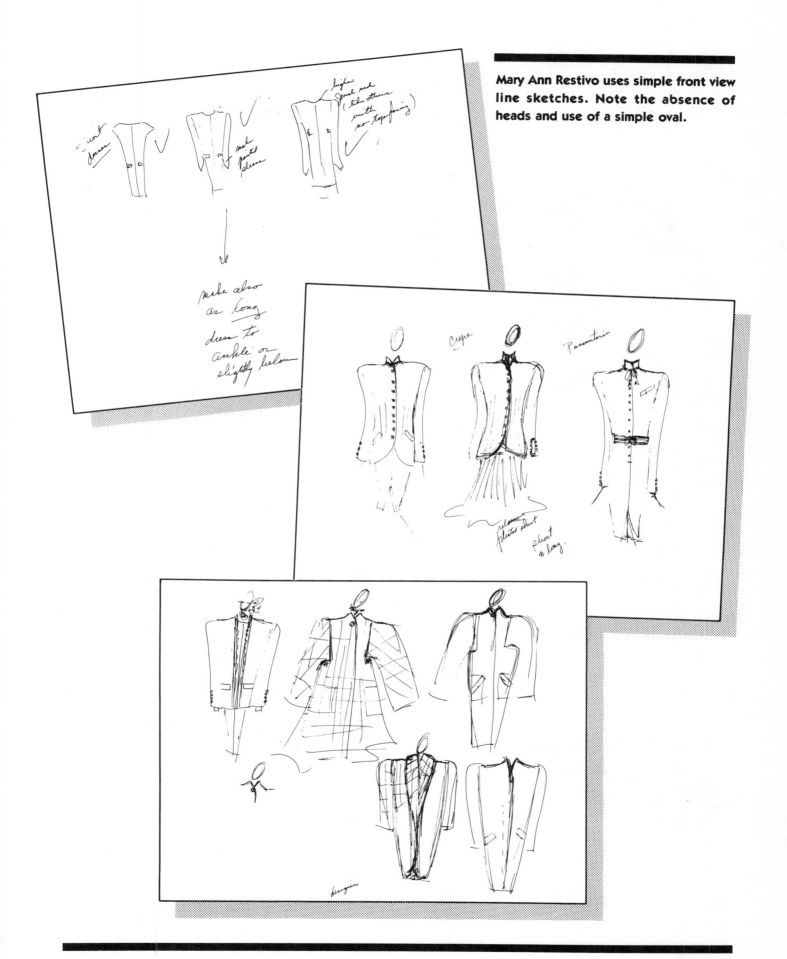

Mary Ann Restivo uses simple front view line sketches. Note the absence of heads and use of a simple oval.

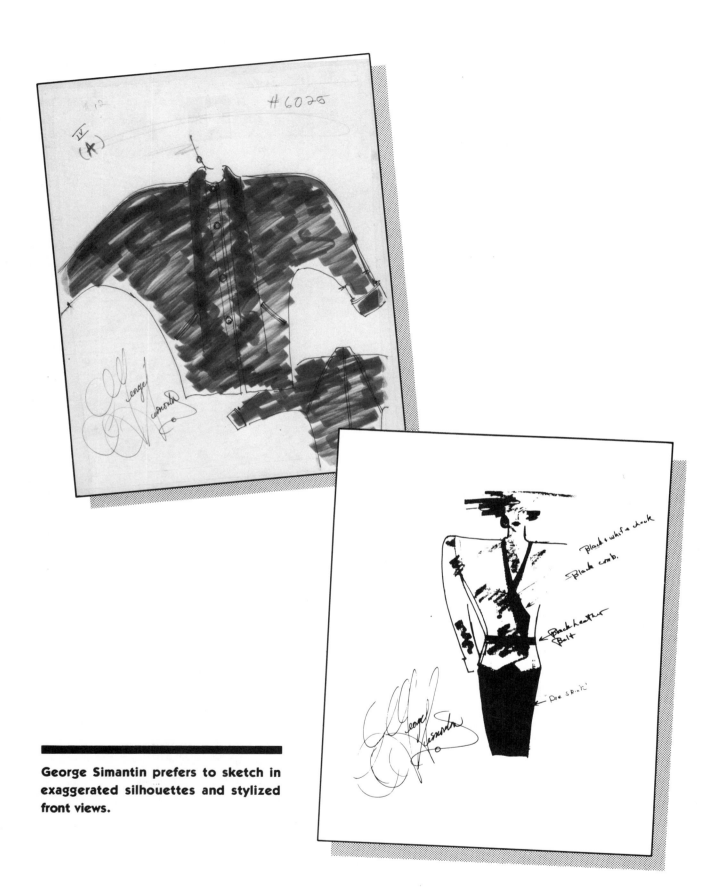

George Simantin prefers to sketch in exaggerated silhouettes and stylized front views.

Monika Tilley (below) does a number of design concept sketches on a single page, while Joan Bellew for Joseph Love Inc. (right) completes each design idea with back view, notes and fabric swatch.

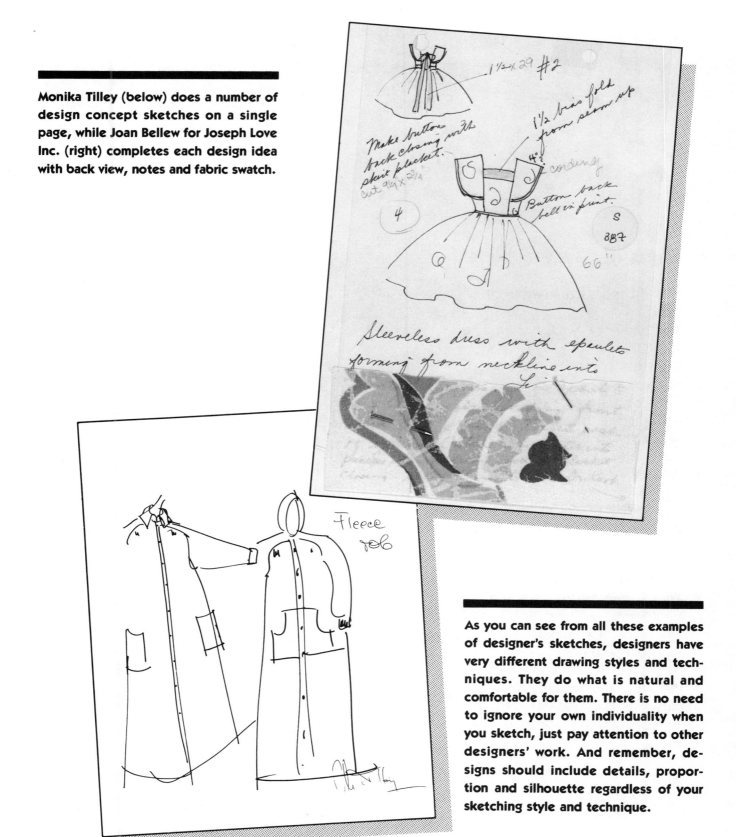

As you can see from all these examples of designer's sketches, designers have very different drawing styles and techniques. They do what is natural and comfortable for them. There is no need to ignore your own individuality when you sketch, just pay attention to other designers' work. And remember, designs should include details, proportion and silhouette regardless of your sketching style and technique.

A designer sees shapes, silhouettes and proportions, and the rhythm and flow of fabric. The process is completed with construction details and trim. The following exercises may be helpful if you want to try your hand at design sketching. But before you start, you must understand fashion proportions, also referred to as a **croqui.**

POINTS TO REMEMBER

◆ The shoulders are wider than the hips.

◆ The hips are wider than the waist.

◆ The wrist comes to the bottom of the torso.

◆ The elbow aligns with the waist.

◆ If the arms are too long, the garment will appear out of proportion.

◆ A larger head will make the figure look younger and a smaller head will make the figure appear more sophisticated.

◆ If a larger or smaller head is taken to an extreme, the figure will be out of proportion.

◆ The knees should be placed between the bottom of the torso and the ankles.

◆ A good fashion figure should be one-half from the top of the head to the bottom of the torso, and one-half from the bottom of the torso to the ankle.

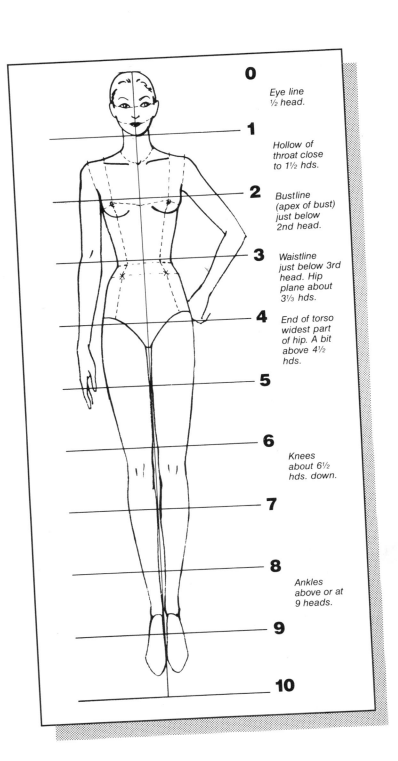

0 — Eye line ½ head.

1 — Hollow of throat close to 1½ hds.

2 — Bustline (apex of bust) just below 2nd head.

3 — Waistline just below 3rd head. Hip plane about 3⅓ hds.

4 — End of torso widest part of hip. A bit above 4½ hds.

5

6 — Knees about 6½ hds. down.

7

8 — Ankles above or at 9 heads.

9

10

Once you are familiar with fashion proportions, you may want to design active sportswear such as for aerobics or gymnastics. These are examples of students' work after two lessons. Note the diversity of ideas and subtle differences in the interpretation of the basic croqui.

DESIGN EXERCISE USING THE SILHOUETTE SHAPE

Supplies needed:

◆ Wide dark gray marker (gray #7 or #8 Design Marker®, white pencil, Prismacolor #938®)
◆ Fine line pen (Pilot®, Stylist®, Le Pen®)
◆ Marker Pad (If you use a paper that bleeds through, put a heavier paper such as bristol board between the sheet you are using and the rest of the pad.)

Now you're ready to begin. Think of shapes . . . triangles, squares, rectangles, ovals, "T", "V". Simplicity is important when you start. Expect some odd-looking creatures. It takes time for the eye and the hand to deliver the message in your mind.

If you want a bit more interest in the pose, move one foot forward and/or change the position of the arms and head.

Imagine that you're in a dark room. There is a large doorway leading into the room from a brightly lit room. A figure enters and stops in the doorway. What shapes do you see? Draw them!

Then use a white pencil to clarify the inner construction and details. (The pencil is also used to make corrections or to sharpen the silhouette.) Remember, the fabric is important, so use your fine line pen for notations.

If you have advanced or more developed art skills, try an action or turned (three-quarter) figure.

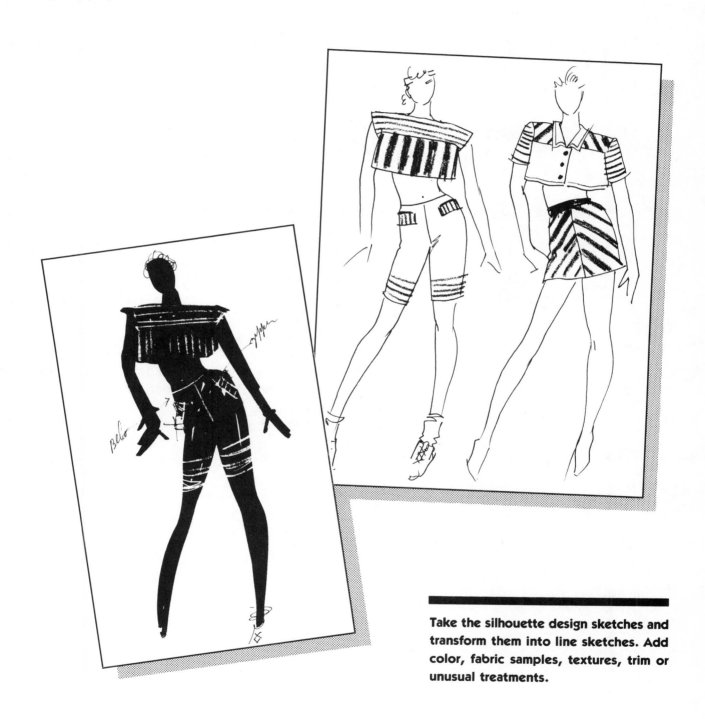

Take the silhouette design sketches and transform them into line sketches. Add color, fabric samples, textures, trim or unusual treatments.

FREE-LANCE DESIGNER

A designer can work for (or own) a firm, and be paid a salary or share in the profits. The staff designer is totally committed to that one firm.

A free-lance designer can service many firms, though they cannot (or should not) be involved with firms producing the same type (or price level) of garments. They are paid by the assignment. Contracts and services vary a great deal. Clearly, arrangements and responsibilities are a matter of agreement between the parties involved and should be discussed before a job begins.

Some free-lancers provide the first sample along with the design sketch. Some work on a retainer basis and deliver a set number of idea sketches on a regular time schedule. There are free-lance designers who are completely responsible for the season's line including designs, shopping the fabric market, sources, cost and elaborate presentation boards. Others work in the company's workroom for specified time periods directing patternmakers and samplehands.

Good clear design sketches usually accompanied by flats, fabrics and notations are part of the free-lancer's design presentation.

Private labels, specialty chains, special interest and licensing groups, manufacturers who do not employ staff designers are among those who retain the free-lance designer.

Free-lance designer Diane DeMers researches the market, trends and colors, and delivers distinctive themes for a knitwear line.

PRELIMINARY PRESENTATIONS

Everyone involved at this stage of the design process uses a method to show their design concepts called a presentation board. These are preliminary presentations where those involved can get an overview of the projected line, and where revisions and changes can be made easily. On the other hand final presentations are more complete, and the art has a more finished quality (see **pages 57—63**).

The preliminary presentation is a continuous process, occuring throughout the design stage, and can be both exhilarating and frustrating.

Many ideas and concepts are considered. Formal and informal meetings are held. Fabrics are considered for their texture, color and cost. A theme can be considered "hot" and then it may evolve into something entirely different, or it may be discarded. Therefore, artwork is usually in a "rough" or "crude" form. These rough ideas and preliminary presentations go through an evolutionary process until the time for decision-making arrives.

These sketches were prepared to give buyers an idea of how designer Ellen Gang's "Varsity" piece would look in garments. Presentations similar to this are often done at Knitwaves, Inc. before the actual fabric is created. Sketches are shown with a printing of the fabric. In this case, when the actual fabric was determined, the styles were changed slightly.

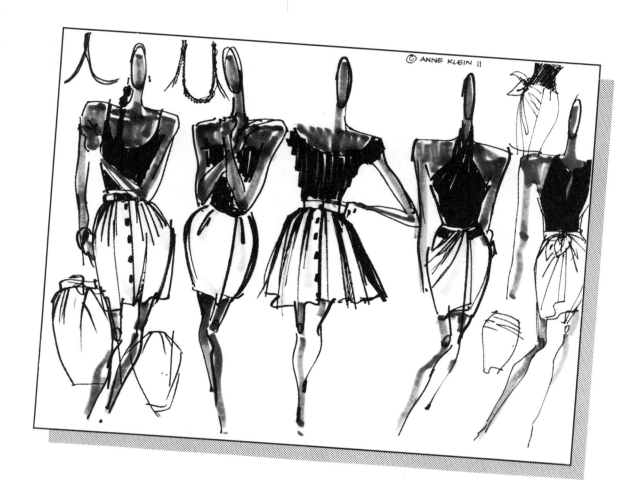

Skirt designs are the main focus in this preliminary presentation from Anne Klein II. Before the final presentation is completed, each skirt design as well as appropriate tops will be clarified and selected.

This was a classroom demonstration to assist students in coordinating fabrics and pieces. Note the simple addition of accessories when they were needed to express a desired "look." Heads and feet are indicated, but not completed at this preliminary stage. Changes are made. There is no limit to the number of pages and sketches done at this time. An editing process follows and pages may be deleted completely, put aside for future use, etc.

THREE

IN-HOUSE PRODUCTION

A design has been selected ... and a metamorphosis occurs ... the design sketch on paper becomes a wearable garment.

Whereas the design stage involves a few individuals, many people are involved in the production of the final product, including design assistant(s), patternmakers, samplehands, graders, cost and production managers, shippers, factory workers, contractors, and those responsible for quality control. Each individual has his/her own duties and plays an important role in the production of the clothes that the consumer sees in window and interior displays, on racks in the stores, in ads, etc. All work is done on a "tight" schedule with deadlines that must be met. All procedures are coordinated to make maximum use of time. Time is money.

The network of visual communication of all these phases of production is crucial. The fashion design sketch helps a great deal. Style numbers and written information are valuable, and the patternmaker, salesperson, cost and production manager, etc., will recognize the garment at a glance from the sketch. The different types of sketches serve a specific function.

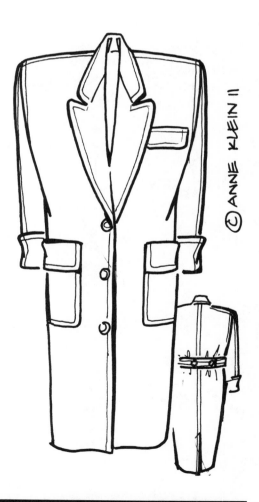

© ANNE KLEIN II

SAMPLE SKETCH
(OR WORKROOM
SKETCH)

A sample sketch is sometimes called a workroom or production sketch. It is used to transform the designer's original sketch into a finished garment. Unlike the creative design sketch, a sample sketch should accurately and clearly show construction details, silhouette and proportion. The back view is also drawn. The sketch is not necessarily stylized or exaggerated. Accessories and hairstyles are not important.

The sample sketch is used by the assistant designer, the samplehand and the patternmaker. The assistant will drape the garment in muslin. The patternmaker will then develop patterns or will make necessary adjustments on existing slopers, which are specific pattern shapes of oaktag or heavy paper. The sample sketch is the source of information and is always on display. A small fabric swatch for the sample is attached to the sketch. Important measurements, for example, the depth of pleats or tucks are always noted.

The fabric selected for the finished garment is cut into the various garment sections and given to the samplehand along with the sample sketch. The various pieces are then sewn together by the sample hand, and the sketch becomes reality. After the garment is sewn, it is placed on a model form or worn by a showroom model. The designer will check to see how closely the design has been interpreted, and will make any adjustments or changes necessary. Throughout this entire process, the sample sketch is the common denominator.

It is important to note at this time that the amount of information given on a sample sketch will vary from manufacturer to manufacturer. Individuals working together will develop their own code. In the process of bringing the design idea to reality, a few easy lines can become a recognized message.

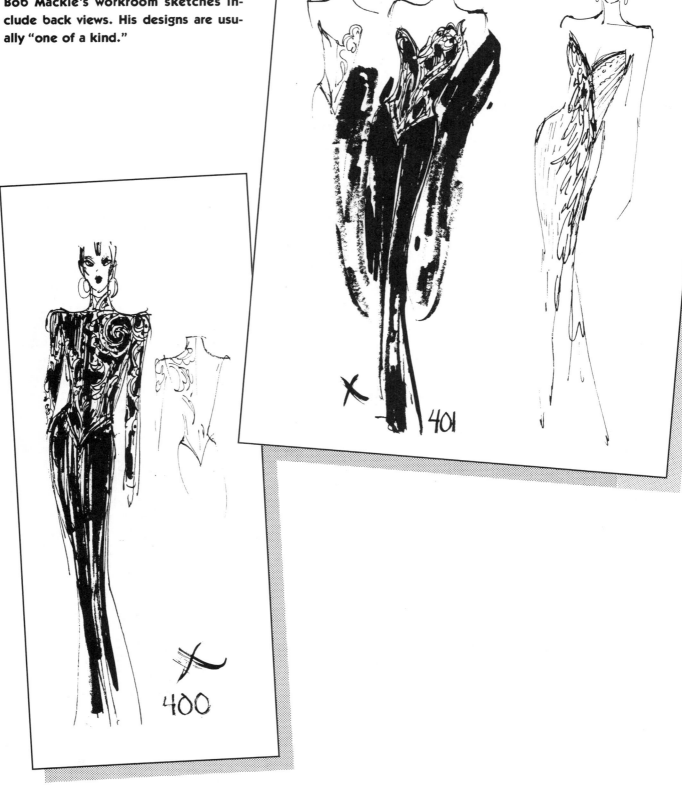

Bob Mackie's workroom sketches include back views. His designs are usually "one of a kind."

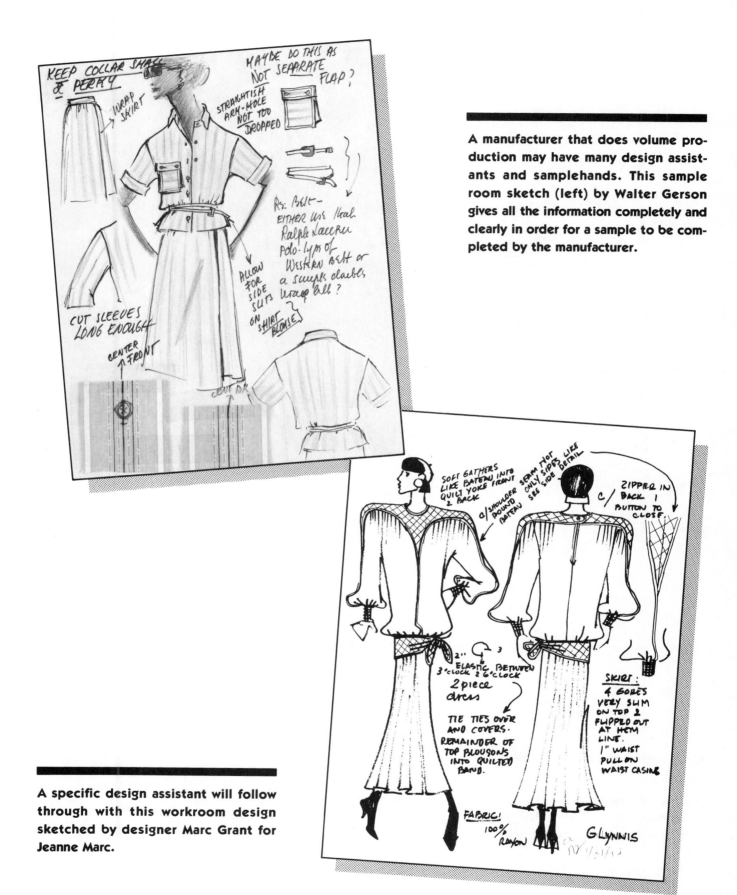

A manufacturer that does volume production may have many design assistants and samplehands. This sample room sketch (left) by Walter Gerson gives all the information completely and clearly in order for a sample to be completed by the manufacturer.

A specific design assistant will follow through with this workroom design sketched by designer Marc Grant for Jeanne Marc.

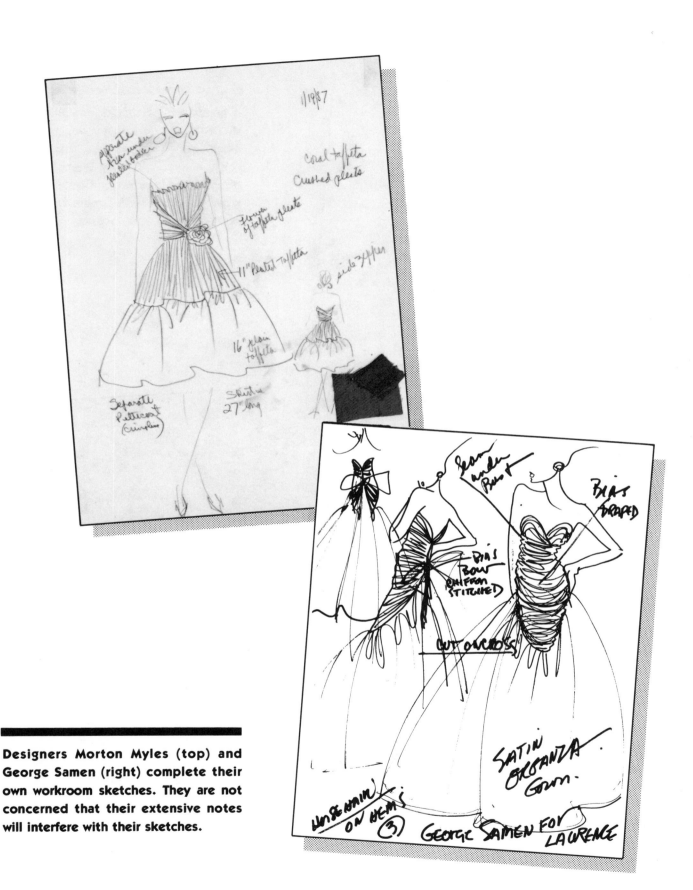

Designers Morton Myles (top) and George Samen (right) complete their own workroom sketches. They are not concerned that their extensive notes will interfere with their sketches.

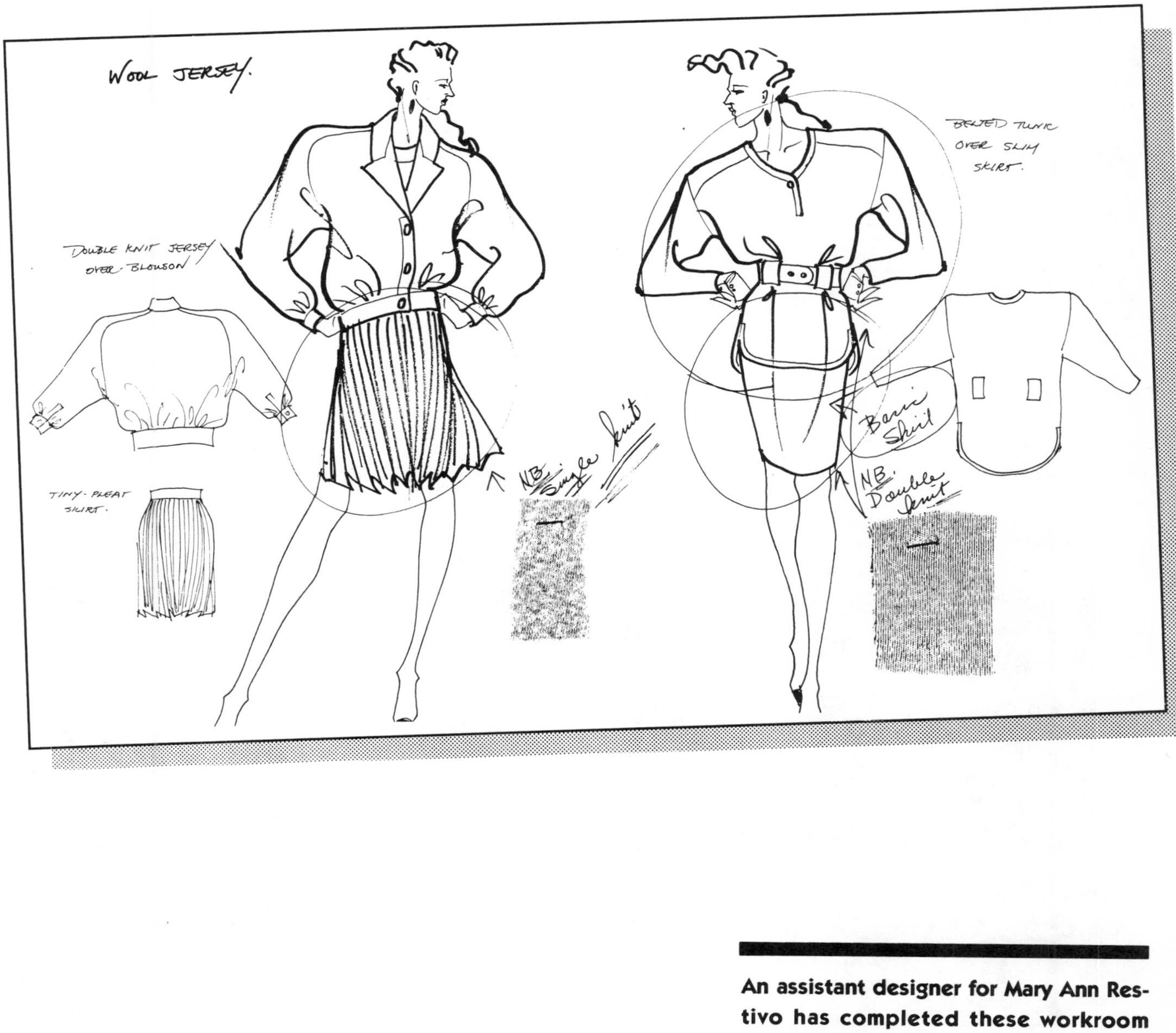
WOOL JERSEY.
DOUBLE KNIT JERSEY OVER BLOUSON
TINY-PLEAT SKIRT.
BELTED TUNIC OVER SLIM SKIRT.
Basic Skirt
NB: Single knit
NB: Double knit

An assistant designer for Mary Ann Restivo has completed these workroom sketches. Of course, Restivo has "ok'd" all changes.

WORKBOARD

A workboard is an important coordinating tool used by many as a form of communication in the business of fashion. It consists of a number of sketches representing a complete line or collection, or a special group of designs. One popular format includes a garment sketch on a piece of paper, approximately 4" by 6". The sketch is a simple front view and numbered. The purpose of the workboard will determine the type of sketch used.

Each firm has their own way of using workboards. In

the design workroom an "X" is sometimes drawn through a sketch when the sample has been completed. Some workboards are used in the planning and execution of the firm's fashion show or season opening. The models, dressers, and commentator can see at a glance the order in which the garments are to be shown as well as what accessories are to be worn with it. Workboards are also used by some firms to assist in keeping records of orders, pieces in production and pieces ready for shipment.

The workboard may be used by fashion show coordinators for the model lineup. There will be no mistake of the order the designer wants the line shown.

A variety of formats are used to complete workboards depending on the area covered. Here, Mary Ann Restivo groups items within categories, e.g. tops, bottoms, dresses.

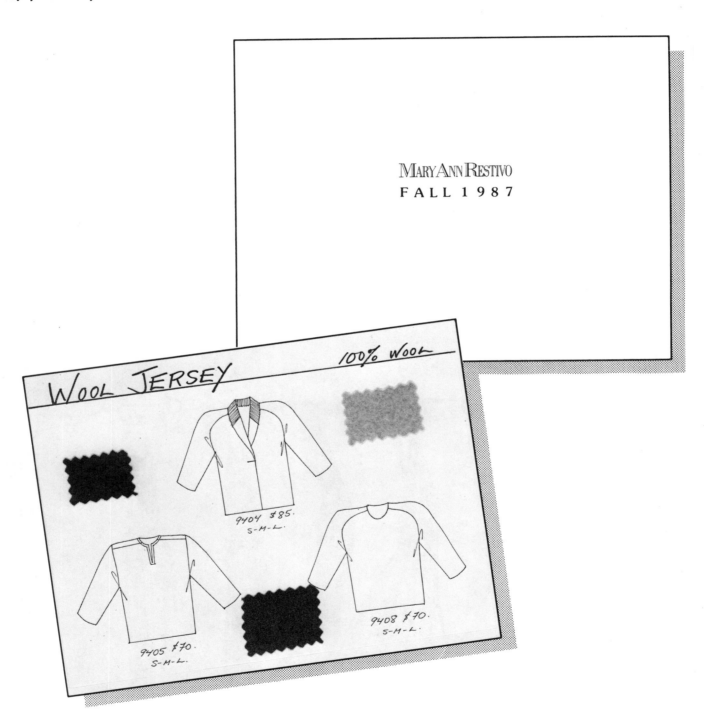

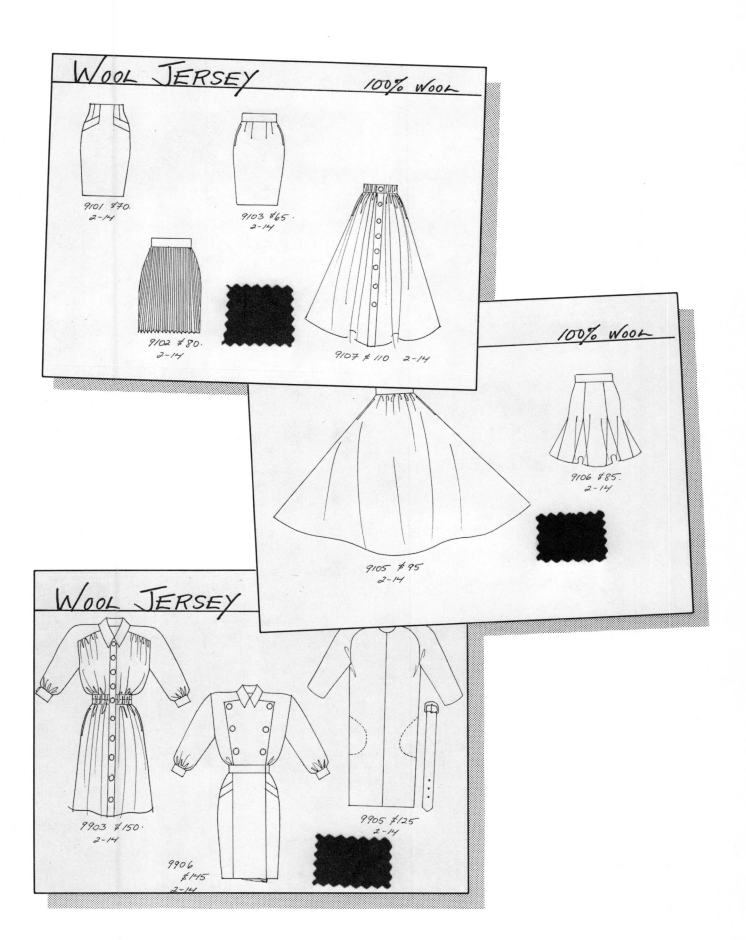

WOOL JERSEY
100% WOOL

9101 $70.
2-14

9103 $65.
2-14

9102 $80.
2-14

9107 $110 2-14

100% WOOL

9106 $85.
2-14

9105 $95
2-14

WOOL JERSEY

9903 $150.
2-14

9906
$145
2-14

9905 $125
2-14

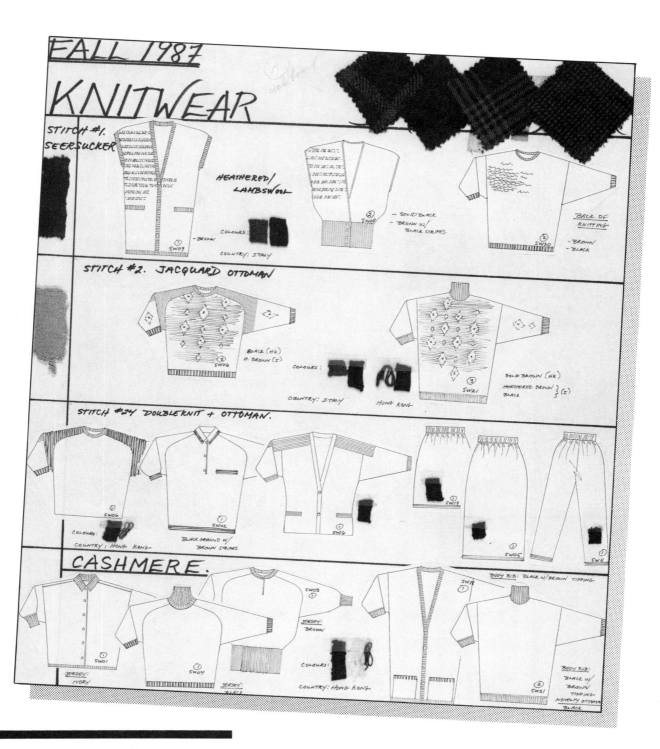

Although many workboards contain garment sketches and fabric swatches, it is not unusual to see sketches and swatches on separate boards. Mary Ann Restivo uses a separate board (facing page) to include all the fabrics proposed for a line.

FLATS, FLOATS, SPECS

Apparel designs are often shown without the figure. They are called flats, floats and specs (specifications). These fashion sketches fill specific needs.

Flats are used primarily to show how the garment looks from the back view. They give necessary information pertaining to construction, details, closures (how to get into and out of the garment). For example, the design in front shows a belted garment with an easy fit (**A**). The back view will show if it is a one-piece loose dress (**B**), or a dress with a set-in waistline and a zipper (**C**), or a two-piece outfit (**D**).

Flats are used for sample room sketches and in pattern-books. A fabric swatch and a back view in the flat completes the design plate. There is no rule that a back view must be shown in the flat.

Floats are fashion drawings also shown without the figure, but the designs are sketched in a more realistic or relaxed manner. Lines are curved and creases are indicated. They are used by forecast services a great deal, and many design ideas are sketched in this manner.

Specs, the shortened term for specifications, are the most important drawing of this group. Every fashion design portfolio should include spec drawings to show the designer's (or applicant's) ability to draw a garment in correct proportion, using accurate measurements. Specs are essential in the production of the garment, especially as more garments are produced overseas.

Following are a wide variety of formats for drawing specs used by different manufacturers. Because the approach and requirements vary, some basic instructions are given following the samples to enable you to complete simple spec drawings using a few, but essential, measurements. The employer will provide you with specific instructions to fulfill that firm's individual needs and requirements.

A   B   C   D

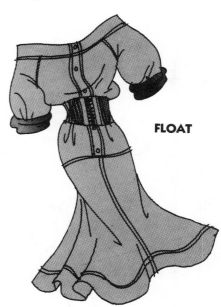

FLOAT

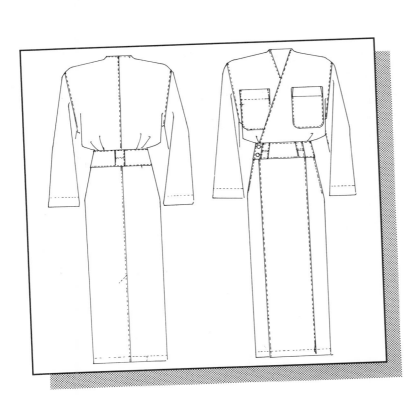

FLAT

You may think that these knitwear designs are clear and complete. Yes, they are . . . for presentation of line. The spec sheet for #1 sketch lists specifically the information needed for volume production.

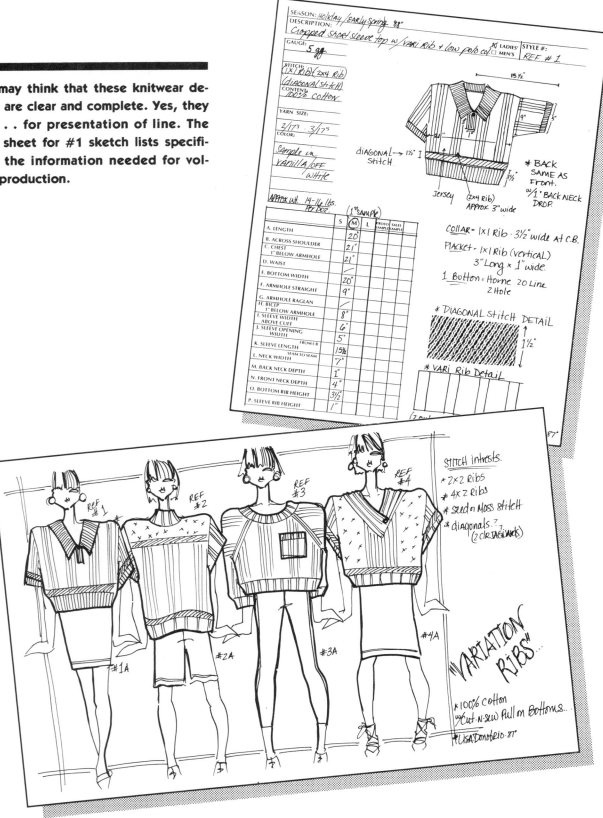

This spec sheet from Carol Horn is accompanied by a graphic pattern for design and color combinations for this jacquard sweater. The original concept was developed from a design for a Viennese pillowcase.

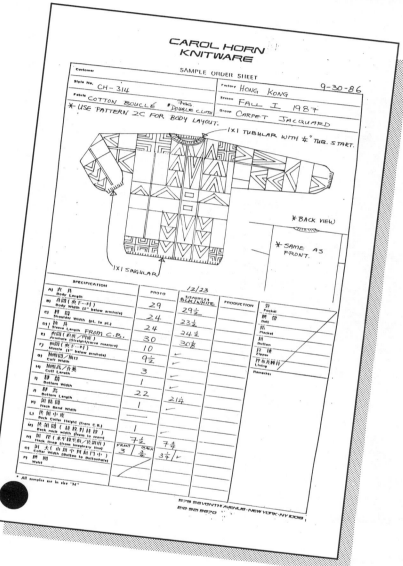

			S	M	L	XL
1. Across shoulders	肩濶					
2. Across back yoke	后裡中長 (3½" from C.B.N.)		17-1/4	18-1/4	19-1/4	20-1/4
3. Back yoke/C.B.N.	后裡十長		16-3/4	17-1/4	18-3/4	19-3/4
4. Drop of front yoke	前裡下長		3-1/2	3-1/2	3-1/2	3-1/2
5. Mid chest (Midpoint of armhole)	甲橫濶					
6. Chest 1" under armhole	胸濶 (夹低下1"度)		15	16	17	18
7. Waist 8" below armhole	腰濶 (夹低下8"度)		19-3/4	21-3/4	23-3/4	25-3/4
8. Bottom opening	脚濶		19-3/4	21-3/4	23-3/4	25-3/4
9. Body length	衣長		19-3/4	21-3/4	23-3/4	25-3/4
10. Armhole	夹圍		31	31-1/2	32	32-1/2
11. Sleeve length	袖長		19-1/2	20-1/2	21-1/2	22-1/2
12. Sleevewidth 1" below armhole	臂濶 (夹低下1"度)		33-1/4	34-1/4	35-1/4	35-1/4
13. Sleevewidth 10" from cuffedge	前臂濶 (介口起上10"度)		8-1/4	8-1/4	9-1/4	9-3/4
14. Sleevewidth 5" from cuffedge	臂濶 (介口起上5"度)		6-1/2	7	7-1/2	8
15. Cuff opening	介末濶		5-3/4	6	6-1/4	6-1/2
16. Height of sleeve cuff	介末高		4-1/4	4-1/2	4-3/4	5
17. Height of hemmed bottom	脚高		2-3/8	2-3/8	2-3/8	2-3/8
18. Collar points	領尖長		2-3/8	2-3/8	2-3/8	2-3/8
19. Collar spread	領安起高		1/8	1/8	1/8	1/8
20. Front placket A) Length	領安濶		2-3/8	2-3/8	2-3/8	2-3/8
B) Width	胸濶					
21. Collar circumference	領圍					
22. Collar height A) Unfold	領上下總高		1-3/8	1-3/8	1-3/8	1-3/8
B) Band	領下幼高		15	16	17	18
23. Pocket A) Finished length	袋高		3-1/4	3-1/4	3-1/4	3-1/4
B) Finished width	袋濶		1-1/2	1-1/2	1-1/2	1-1/2
24. Pocket position A) Shoulder	袋口至頂起點		5-1/4	5-1/4	5-1/4	5-1/4
B) Buttonhole 袋内領至胸门高			4-5/8	4-5/8	4-5/8	4-5/8
25. Pocket Hemming A) Height			8-1/4	8-1/2	8-3/4	9
B)			1	2-1/4	1	2-3/4
26. Sleeve placket A) Length 袖衩长				1	1	1
B) Width 袖衩濶			7	7	7	7
27. Epaulet A) Length 肩挥長			1	1	1	7...
B) Width 肩挥濶			1	1	1	1
28. Sideseam Length						
			18	18	18	18

Notes : 1), Collar No. 300 Classic   Neckband No. 95.   2) Folded Pack.
3) Button: Rochester AP-1725 Ecru 16L.

Check Box for
Stitch Type

Edge Stitch Type	Collar	Placket	Pocket	Pocket-Flap	Shoulder	Armhole	Cuff	Side seam	Epaulet	Bottom	Back yoke
¼ or ⅛ Topstitch	X		X								
Double					X						
Felled										X	
Single Needle							X				
Other											
		X				X		X			

Prepared by _____ A. Supervisor _____ M. Approved by _____

Bill Blass No. BS16196   Fabric Design No. #5160
Description Men's top-fused collar L/S shirts,
                1-3/8" top-center, 1 button-thru round pocket.
Content 55% Cotton Yarn Size _____ Construction _____
        45% Poly   Gauge _____
Care: Hand Wash _____ Dry Clean _____ Stitch/Inch 15-16
      Machine Wash x   Shrinkage _____ Other _____

A typical format for overseas production. Information is included in English and in the contracting host's language.

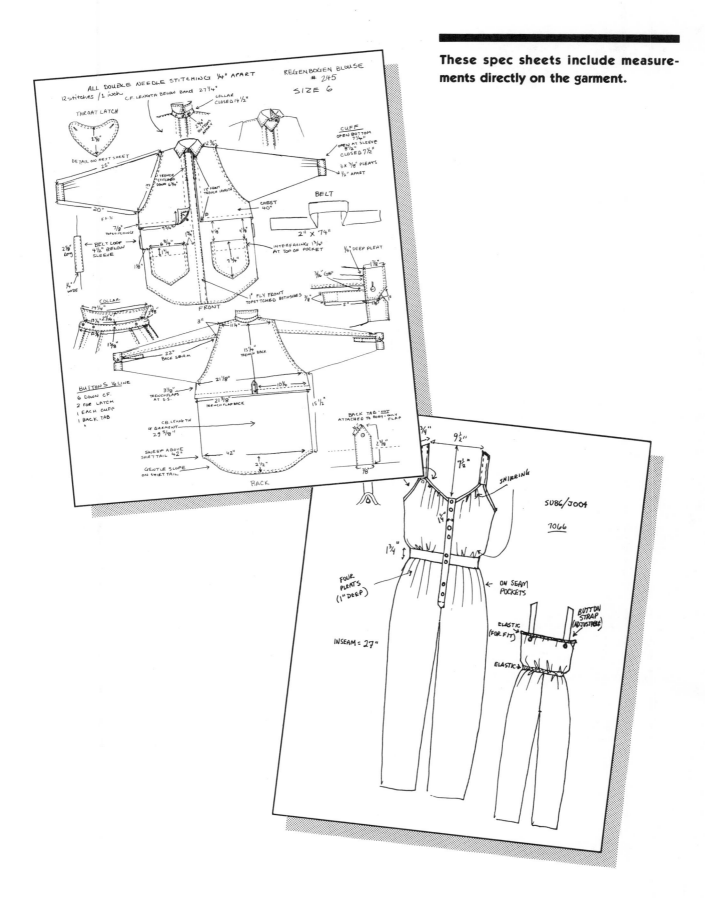

These spec sheets include measurements directly on the garment.

SPEC DRAWINGS

Supplies needed:

- ◆ Graph paper . . . approximately 5 squares to 1 inch
- ◆ Ruler . . . plastic see-through is preferred
- ◆ 2B or #2 sharpened pencils
- ◆ Medium-line pen
- ◆ Marker or layout paper . . . If you use heavier paper, you will need a light box in order to transfer the spec guide into the spec drawing.

Our first objective is to prepare spec guides for tops (blouses, shirts, jackets), bottoms (skirts, pants), and coats and dresses. Spec guides vary with the specific needs. However, all pieces must appear in proportion to each other, so we start with the complete figure (**A**). As previously discussed head, hands, and feet are not drawn when we spec a garment, although they are used in the preparation of spec guides.

Working in pencil, complete a figure using graph paper, making sure both sides are even.

1. Using the top part of the figure (to bottom of torso), complete spec guide for lightweight top pieces (shirts, blouses) (**B**).
2. Repeat the process for heavier or outerwear garments, broadening the shoulders and continuing spec guide length desired (**C**).
3. The spec guide for pants (shorts, etc.) requires a guide with legs slightly apart (**E**).

Remember, variations must be equal on both sides. Graph paper makes this a simple task. Add helpful guidelines.

If you're satisfied with the spec guides drawn, go over the pencil lines with a pen (kneaded eraser will help remove pencil marks).

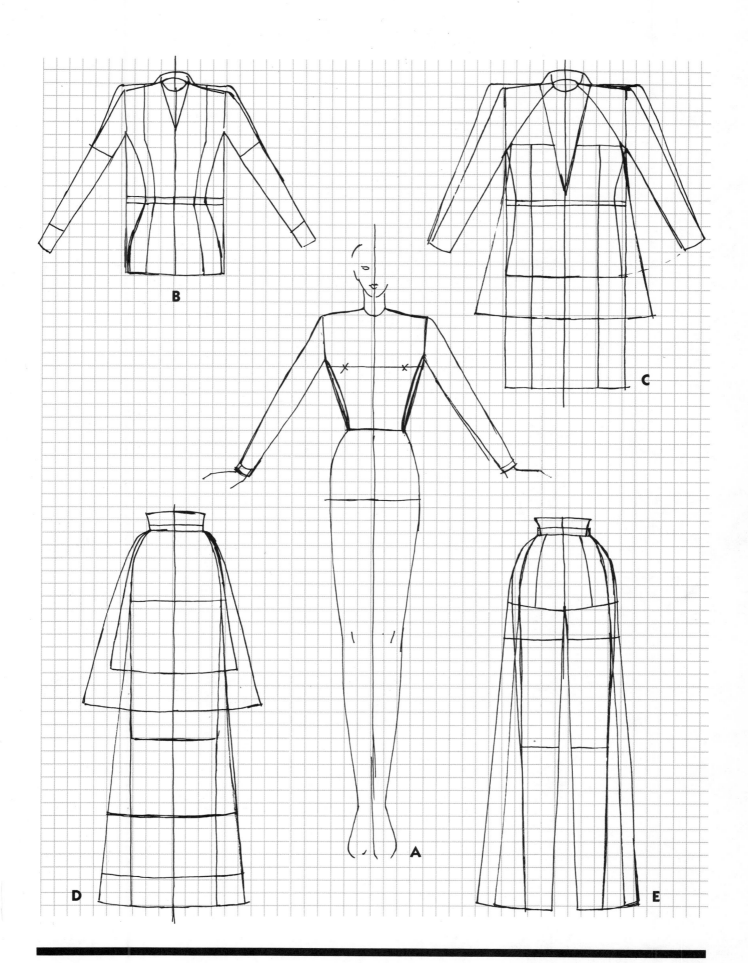

B

C

A

D

E

In order to show exactly what part of the garment the measurements relate to, draw two short lines (**a**) and a line from each ending with an arrow and with a break in the middle (**b**). Write the measurement in this space (**c**).

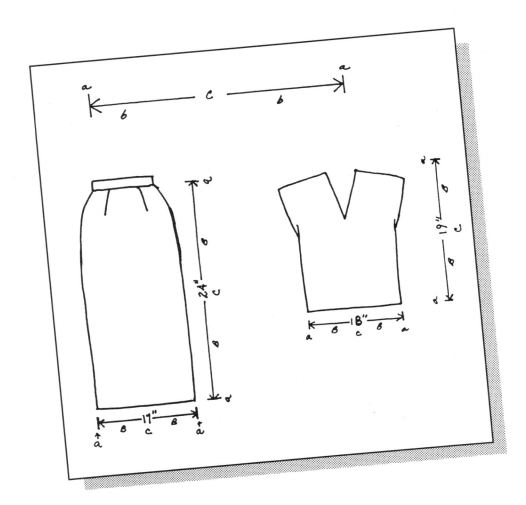

Now for the fun part, adding the measurements. Where do you get them from? Which ones do you use? Is it important to show the sleeve length? How do you indicate them?

◆ **For Tops**
   Length—from back of the neck to hemline
   Width—from side seam to side seam at hemline
◆ **For Skirts**
   Length—from waist to the hemline
   Width—from side seam to side seam at hemline
◆ **For Pants**
   Length—from waist to the hemline
   Width—(one leg) from side seam to side seam

Remember, your spec guides are very important to you. Guide shapes used are a matter of choice. Once you have a set of guide specs with measurements, you will need very little time to spec an individual piece. However, if you are doing a sweater line or a group of daytime dresses, you may want to prepare a special spec guide.

Now you are ready to test the waters. Design a three-piece outfit, showing the total look on a figure. The pose and technique are of your individual choosing. Spec each piece on the same page.

Check the proportions between the fashion sketch and the specs. Does the sleeve length relate to the jacket length? How is the armhole seam constructed? Is the ratio of the width and length of the garment the same? Etc.

Once you can draw specs properly, you will always design fashion thinking of measurements and proportions.

The illustrations here and on the following page are examples of students' assignments in preparing spec guides. Note the measurements on the drawings.

HELPFUL HINTS

- ◆ A straight skirt is the same width at the hips as at the hemline. If the hip measurement is 34″, the skirt will measure 17″ from side seam to side seam.
- ◆ A blouse will measure from the back of the neck to the waist (17″) plus the amount needed to tuck in (7″). A total of 24″.
- ◆ The average showroom model is a size 8 or 10 and about 5′7″ tall.

PRESENTATIONS

In the preliminary presentation concepts, styles and fabrics are considered and discarded; themes and ideas are explored. The presentations at this level are not polished or considered final. No firm commitment has been established.

A finished presentation on the other hand is planned when all the decisions regarding a design line, group or collection have been completed. More attention is paid to the art at this time. The garment is illustrated on the fashion figure, and appropriately accessorized. Fabric swatches are included either with the sketch or separately. When back views are shown, they are in the flat form. Pieces are placed in separate categories, e.g., tops, skirts. There are usually a number of presentations to make up that season's line.

Conferences take place to review the completed presentation. It is unlikely that any major changes will occur at this time. Parties representing the financial, marketing and business factions of a firm often are present. Advertising and promotion are among the topics discussed and planned when reviewing the presentations. Schedules and budgets are developed.

Any student aspiring to enter the fashion industry as a designer should plan a portfolio along the lines of a finished or final presentation.

Final presentation for a fall line of pants and blouses. The basic silhouette does not change, however the details vary. Notice the variety of necklines and waistlines.

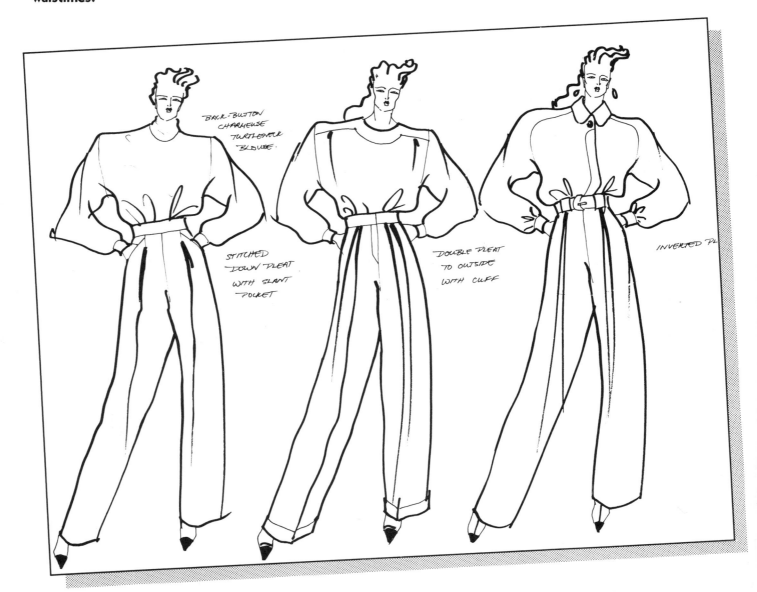

BACK-BUTTON
CHARMEUSE
TURTLENECK
BLOUSE.

STITCHED
DOWN PLEAT
WITH SLANT
POCKET

DOUBLE PLEAT
TO OUTSIDE
WITH CUFF

INVERTED PL

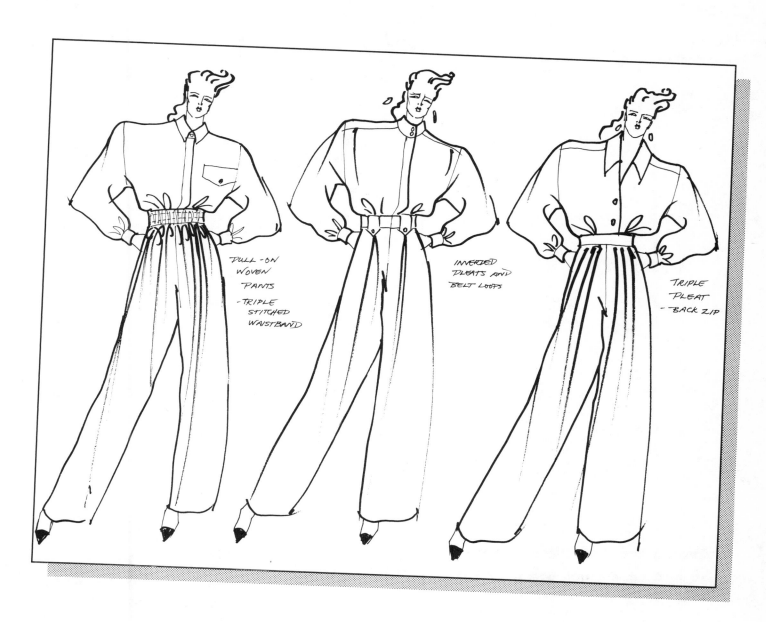

PULL-ON
WOVEN
PANTS

-TRIPLE
STITCHED
WAISTBAND

INVERTED
PLEATS AND
BELT LOOPS

TRIPLE
PLEAT
- BACK ZIP

Two final presentation boards from Betty Hanson & Co. include line sketches, color illustrations and fabric swatches. Note the mix of prints, stripes and solids.

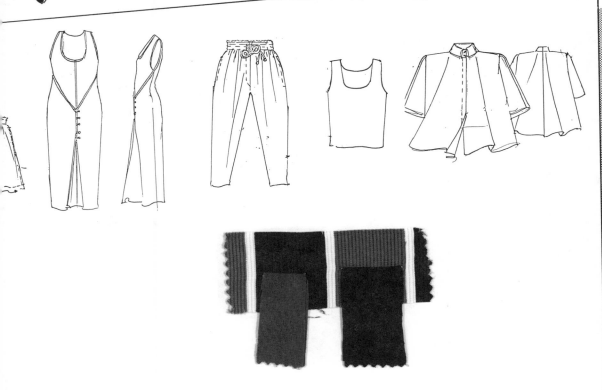

A versatile summer line from Joseph Vincent. It is easy to see the inter-changeable garment parts in this final presentation.

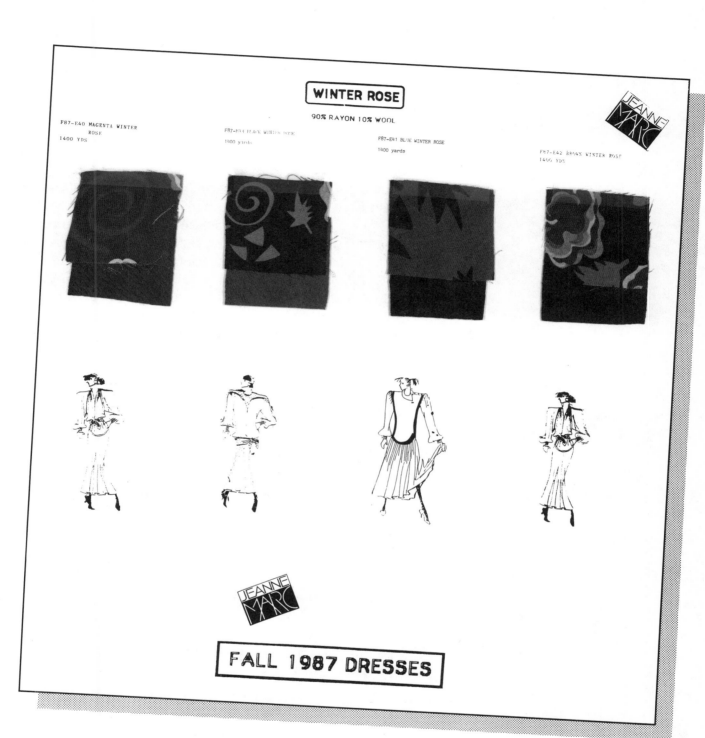

WINTER ROSE

90% RAYON 10% WOOL

F87-E40 MAGENTA WINTER
ROSE
1400 YDS

F87-E43 BLACK WINTER ROSE
1400 yards

F87-E41 BLUE WINTER ROSE
1400 yards

F87-E42 BROWN WINTER ROSE
1400 YDS

FALL 1987 DRESSES

Jeanne Marc designs their own fabrics and uses this type of board for final presentations. A small copy of the design sketch is included with a large fabric swatch.

RECORDKEEPING ART

All firms keep records relating to business performance. Everyone is aware of financial reports, accounts receivable and payable. In the fashion industry, a "visual" record is also kept of the apparel produced.

After a line has been completed, a record is kept of the garments sold during that season. The recordkeeping sketch consists of a style number of the garment, usually on the figure, a back view and a fabric swatch. Other pertinent information may include fabric content and source, trim, dates, volume, areas sold, etc. A firm may hire a fashion illustrator specifically to execute this record-keeping art or they may use the design or workroom sketch.

Recordkeeping serves an immediate and important function. When a new talent joins a firm, whether as executive vice president in charge of sales, or as a designer, they will need background and current information about the firm. Recordkeeping files can be used as a history of the organization as well as a barometer for the future. They clearly show what was sold, where, wholesale costs, and fabric sources. A "hot number" can be carried over into the next season's line with appropriate changes. If a style performed poorly, the records can help avoid a repetition.

Recording fashion in this manner tells us much about the era in which the clothing was produced. The art or drawing techniques, accessories and hairstyles as well as figure proportions become available for research and study. Authors use these visual records for material when writing about the history of fashion and costume. Record-keeping books and files are considered valuable and can be found in libraries, museums, with collections devoted to fashion.

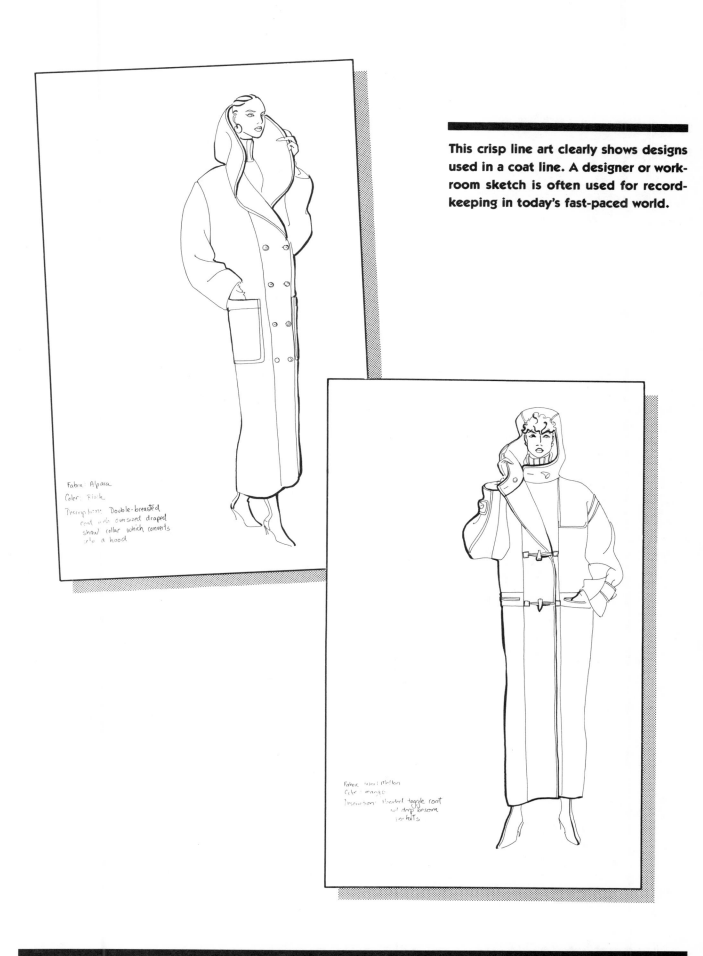

This crisp line art clearly shows designs used in a coat line. A designer or workroom sketch is often used for record-keeping in today's fast-paced world.

Fabric: Alpaca
Color: Flink
Description: Double-breasted coat with oversized draped shawl collar which converts into a hood

Fabric: Wool Melton
Color: mango
Description: Hooded toggle coat w/ deep besom pockets

Recordkeeping art from the past decades reflect not only the styles of clothing, but different proportions, looks and techniques. Compare these examples from 1914, 1955, 1966.

April 1st, 1914 92
Black Satin Charmeuse
Trimmed Royal Blue.

#63 "Petrouschka"
Black and white stripe taffeta afternoon gown. G.G.

ORIGINAL BY *Frederic L. Milton*

536
110⁷⁵

547
345⁰⁰

FOUR

MERCHANDISING

To be considered successful a product must sell and make a profit. Yes, there are people who paint lovely landscapes, cook gourmet dishes or build fine furniture. They are successful in their endeavors, and derive a great deal of personal satisfaction from their accomplishments. But if they want to sell their product, they must find a customer to buy it. Finding the customer for their product is called marketing. Merchandising is the term given to marketing a product.

Whether it is to sell a Broadway show, a book or automobile, a new restaurant or a political candidate, reaching the appropriate audience is important. In the fashion industry, fashion art plays a major role in reaching this audience.

The following section explores the various ways fashion art is used to merchandise fashion by manufacturers, the couture or custom design house, resident buying offices, in editorials and in newspapers, magazines and catalogues. There is much more to fashion merchandising than the department store ad, which ultimately (and hopefully) brings the customer in to purchase their goods.

SHOWING
THE LINE

Planning an opening to show the line is an exciting and hectic experience. Openings can take place in a hotel ballroom as an extravagant production or in a small showroom of the manufacturer. They are often covered by the press. Video productions and television are growing forms of media used to publicize these events.

Designers and their firms plan advertising promotions and campaigns to receive maximum coverage. Fashion art is a strong tool used extensively for this purpose.

Specialized publications list the schedules for time and dates to avoid conflicts. This time period is often referred to as market week. Buyers are very busy during this time trying to cover as many openings as possible. Many openings require an invitation and programs are made available at the time of the showings. These elements may require the use of fashion art.

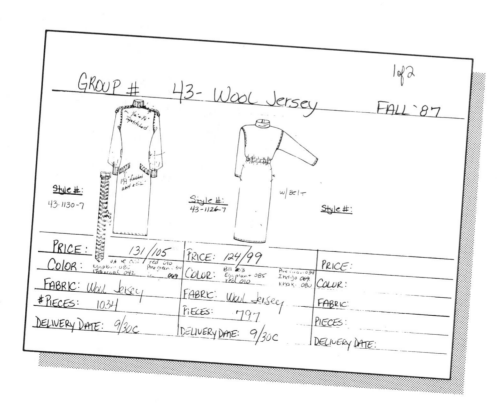

Many firms prepare the type of sheet illustrated on the facing page for the buyer to use in the showroom in conjunction with the actual garment. Other fashion firms print catalogues or folders for the opening of their new lines. Here we see a detailed description and wholesale price list of each item in the firm's line.

NORBURY AND OSUNA
N E W   Y O R K

GROUP I

00% Cotton Jersey
Colors: Navy/Ecru Stripe, Lilac/Ecru Stripe, Solid Navy, Solid Ecru

202	Empire Baby Doll, Jersey dress, long – navy stripe, lilac stripe	$145
204	Full Skirt, Jersey striped gathered skirt, short – navy stripe, lilac stripe, solid navy	$ 90
'05	Baby Doll T-Shirt, Off-the-shoulder cotton striped jersey t-shirt, empire shape – navy stripe, lilac stripe	$ 85
07	Off-The-Shoulder T-Shirt, Striped cotton jersey t-shirt, sleeveless – navy stripe, lilac stripe, solid ecru	$ 85
'07	Off-The-Shoulder T-Shirt, Long sleeve – navy stripe, lilac stripe, solid navy	$ 95
0	Two-Tier Full Empire Dress, Two-tiered gathered empire tent dress with long sleeves and jewel neckline – navy stripe, lilac stripe, solid navy	$240
	Stripe T-Shirt, Long sleeve boat neck striped t-shirt – navy stripe, lilac stripe	$ 90
	Jersey Tango Dress, Ecru trim, bias off-the-shoulder collar, fitted torso with circle flounce, long sleeve – navy stripe, lilac stripe, solid navy, solid ecru	$150
	Jersey Flounce Skirt, Fitted skirt with circle flounce – solid navy, solid ecru	$ 90
	Bell Flounce Dress, Fitted bell dress with ecru collar and cuffs, gold buttons – solid navy	$195
	Full Bubble Skirt, Striped bubble skirt – navy stipe, lilac stripe	$130
	Trapeze Dress, Solid jersey mock turtleneck trapeze shape – solid navy, solid ecru	$150
	Flowers, Striped jersey flowers to accessorize collection	$ 12

Anne Klein II prepares sketches of the highlights (or trendsetters) in their new line, and include in a folder. Buyers, fashion editors and guests receive a copy. Notice how full-size back views are included in some sketches.

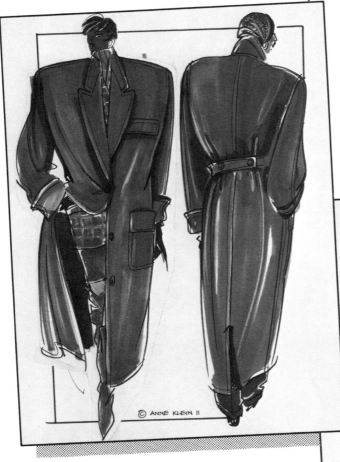

Banana Republic sends catalogues in the mail to their customers. These illustrations clearly represent the type of "safari" image they wish to project.

SELLING THROUGH THE SKETCH

Designs are often sold directly from the sketch. Therefore, the quality, technique and details of the drawings are extremely important. The sketches will vary a great deal depending on the artist's ability and style.

Higher-price couture and custom-made houses depend heavily on the fashion sketch to sell their designs. Their private clientele includes socialites, leaders in business and politics, and celebrities in the entertainment industry. Designs for the theater, opera, ballet, and movies are also selected from the design sketch. Wedding gowns as well as gowns worn by the bridal party are often selected in this manner.

The salesperson often uses the sketch when calling on a client outside of the showroom or in the showroom when the original or duplicate garment is not available. On a much smaller scale, dressmakers will sell a design using a sketch.

Charles Contreri and Wallace Sloves, Ltd. are known for their line of gowns for the bride and her bridal party as well as evening wear. These sketches are used to show the garments to their clients.

#1308

World famous Bob Mackie designs for socialites and entertainment stars using this type of sketch.

BUYING
SERVICES

Buying services are also referred to as resident buying houses. They act as a "middle man" between those producing the garment and those selling at retail level. Throughout the country, there are stores, small and large, chains or individually owned, that cannot or choose not to make their purchases directly from manufacturers or design showrooms. They purchase their inventory through a buying service.

This is another area where the fashion sketch is used extensively to illustrate merchandise available. Vital information is included with the sketch so that the retailer can make a decision as to what to order. The source is listed along with the style number, wholesale price, volume requirements, sizes and colors available, and delivery dates.

Depending on the time of year and type of buying service, material such as catalogues, flyers and bulletins are sent with the relevant information to those subscribing to the service.

Resident buying services such as Independent Retailers Syndicate include sketches with pertinent information to keep their customers—the retailers—informed.

SPORTSWEAR

SUFT SEPARATES SELL

Items are key to Holiday sales and HELENE ST MARIE has the right look at the right price. Tissue faille, solid and novelty metallics, skin jacquards and "palace silk" separates make this line a must-shop resource. Pictured here is a beautiful cummerbund full skirt and patterned metallic top.

Country of origin: U.S.A.

#2025 - Rayon/metallic novelty pattern, S.S. T-body, padded shoulders, keyhole back.
Colors: Assorted Multi Patterrs
Sizes: S-N-L
Cost: $29.00

#2001 - 100% poly tissue faille, soft pleat full skirt with cummerbund waist, back button, back zip.
Colors: Black
Sizes: 4-16
Cost: $32.00

DEPT:
MERCHANDISE: BETTER SPORTSWEAR
RESOURCE: Related Separates
TERMS: HELENE ST MARIE
                      Net
                      mplete
                      les, Cal.
                      PARKS

SPORTSWEAR

PRETTY BLOUSES

Lucky Winner's blouses for Holiday are "pretty". Lace trim "Romance" blouses a winner. T-body pongee prints, dobbies with ribbed waistbands, dobby soft blouses and embroidery trim all at incentive prices.

#8627

#8560

DEPT: Main Floor Sportswear
MERCHANDISE: Blouses
RESOURCE: LUCKY WINNER
TERMS: 8/10 EOM
DELIVERY: Dublin, VA
F.O.B.:   9/1 - 10/30 Cpl
DEPT. HEAD: Bill Friedman
BUYER: Rita Childs
NUMBER: 4-2-4577-4
DATE: 8/12/86 amw

(OVER PLEASE)

EDITORIAL
& SHOWROOM
ART

What is the difference between a fashion design sketch and a fashion illustration? In a design sketch, a designer is translating an idea and is concerned with how the garment is fabricated, constructed and produced. An illustrator is not concerned with how the garment came into being but in showing the finished garment in the most advantageous manner. There is no question that many designers can sketch. Most professional illustrators do not have the skills required of a designer.

Editorial and showroom art is exciting and challenge for the fashion artist.

Showroom art is used in the showroom and relates only to that firm's designs. Art displayed is selected by the firm. It captures the essence or feeling of the garment, and does not necessarily include construction details. It creates an atmosphere, a mood and is used to entice the buyer as they view the firm's product. A fashion illustrator is sometimes hired to execute the drawings. At times the designer's original sketch is used when it has just the right personal touch. Sometimes art used for promotion may also be displayed.

Editorial art accompanies articles written on fashion whether it is an article reporting on fashion or an editor's opinion. The editor selects the artist or requests the art. There are many specialized magazines and newspapers, such as WWD, "The Fashion of the Times" section in the New York Times that employ their own illustrators specifically for the purpose of fashion reporting. Individual design firms also may provide illustrations for the purpose of editorializing.

Many examples of superb fashion art transcend the editorial areas into the realm of fine art. Among the top fashion illustrators in this category are Erté, Joe Eula, Bouché, Eric, Antonio and Kenneth Paul Block.

Note the difference between these Bob Mackie illustrations and his sketches on page 77. The essence of his famous clients is captured in these pieces used as showroom art.

These illustrations were prepared by Carlos Correa, assistant designer for Harvé Benard, to present the new sportswear line to their customers. They are displayed in their showroom. Compare these illustrations with Bob Mackie's on page 81.

Jeanne Marc completes this sketch with background and logo. It is then framed and used in a group to decorate the showroom walls.

NEWSPAPER
& MAGAZINE
ILLUSTRATIONS

Newspaper and magazine illustrations are used to reach the consumer. The buyers determine the item(s) they want to promote and sell. The art department selects the artist. You see ads and recognize the store by the artwork.

There are staff artists within the store's organization, but the better known, higher paid illustrators are free lance. Many have agents.

There are many specialized magazines, newspapers and publications that service both the fashion industry and the buying public.

LACROIX'S FLYING TRAPEZE

WWD
READY-TO-WEAR REPORT

STORES FORECAST A TOUGH YEAR, SCANTY GAINS

A NATIONAL SURVEY

Not seduced by stronger-than-expected Christmas sales, retail industry executives are looking for a lukewarm improvement in 1989 with gains mostly in the 4 to 6 percent range.

They see no letup in competition and expect the rash of takeovers to continue.

On the bright side, they are heartened by the tentative turnaround in the women's apparel business and point out that last year's lackluster sales will enhance this year's comparisons.

"I think 1989 will be very much like 1988 — tough and competitive. We'll get increases in sales and profits, but they won't be great in terms of comp stores," said Bruce G. Allbright, president of Dayton Hudson Corp. in Minneapolis.

"Consumers continue to be demand-

See RETAIL, page 4

PARIS — He helped launch the pervasive pyramid silhouette. And now Christian Lacroix's favorite flying-trapeze looks are going center-ring for spring. Here, sketched exclusively for WWD, his ... gauze and mustard silk ... shiny blue organza

IN THE GYM

Sure, there's arts & crafts after lunch, swimming and canoeing in the lake and ghost stories around the campfire at night. But the main reason 1,000 little girls trooped off to Lake Owen, Wisc. this summer was gymnastics. Six hours of workouts are offered daily.

With women gymnasts dazzling audiences at recent

Doug Rosenthal uses a sensitive line and wash technique for his illustration (facing page) in a fall fashion forecast by Milliken. Simple art (right) is used to accompany an article on children's active wear. Designer Christian Lacroix's original sketch for his 1989 couture collection enhanced the front page of _WWD_ (top).

Fashion related magazines often use well-known illustrators. Here, *American Fabrics & Fashions* highlights an issue with illustrator Antonio.

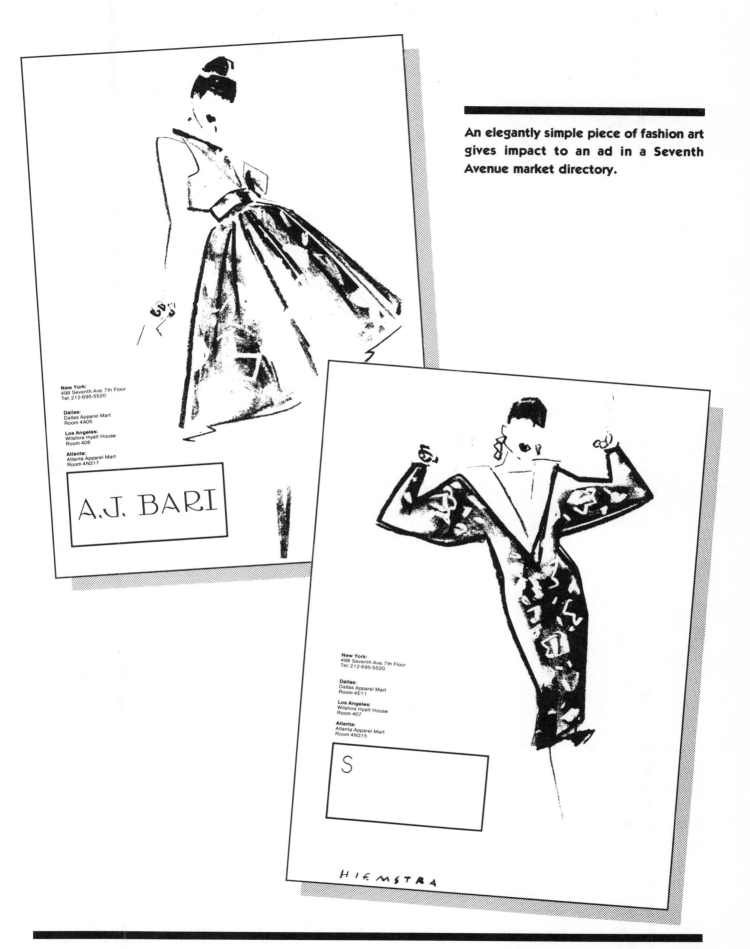

An elegantly simple piece of fashion art gives impact to an ad in a Seventh Avenue market directory.

New York:
498 Seventh Ave. 7th Floor
Tel: 212-695-5520

Dallas:
Dallas Apparel Mart
Room 4A05

Los Angeles:
Wilshire Hyatt House
Room 406

Atlanta:
Atlanta Apparel Mart
Room 4N317

A.J. BARI

New York:
498 Seventh Ave. 7th Floor
Tel: 212-695-5520

Dallas:
Dallas Apparel Mart
Room 4E11

Los Angeles:
Wilshire Hyatt House
Room 407

Atlanta:
Atlanta Apparel Mart
Room 4N315

S

HIEMSTRA

FALL/WINTER
'87/'88

MARCH 15-17
SUNDAY 10 AM to 7 PM
MONDAY 9 AM to 7 PM
TUESDAY 9 AM to 6 PM

DONNA
MODA

AT THE NEW YORK PRET • JACOB K. JAVITS CONVENTION CENTER
FOR TRADE AND PRESS ONLY • INFORMATION: ITALIAN TRADE COMMISSION

SPRING-SUMMER 88

Three days
in September
that shape
fashion's future.

The business
of style,
unmatched and unparalleled,
first and enduring.

THE PULSE OF FASHION.

NEW YORK
PRÊT

SEPTEMBER 13-15, 1987

JACOB K. JAVITS CONVENTION CENTER

FOR INFORMATION CALL AETEC
AMERICAN EUROPEAN TRADE & EXHIBITION CENTER CORP.
225 WEST 34th STREET, SUITE 906, NEW YORK, NY 10122
TEL: (212) 563-5350 TELEX: 6973242 euroamf FAX: (212) 563-4867

OPEN TO THE TRADE AND PRESS ONLY

These stylized suggestions with strong contrasts are often used to attract those in the industry to trade shows. They appeared in the fashion-industry newspaper, *WWD*.

Advertising departments and buyers plan strategies to use the most effective format in order to sell their product. The following pages will illustrate a variety of ads used by different retailers. In all the ads the type of customer targeted is evident. Here, Bonwit Teller uses one cropped figure in a full-page newspaper ad to emphasize "a new approach."

BONWIT TELLER
A NEW APPROACH

Have a long look. Ralph Lauren's striped silks do!

Longer and lovlier. Stretched out. The glorious lineal look that no one does like Ralph Lauren. Even he has never done it before with quite this elegance, this ease. With his black and white striped spectator silks, you move easily into almost any scene. In the top, 378.00. And the skirt, 498.00. Both for 4 to 12 sizes. Ralph Lauren, Second Floor. Trump Tower/57th Street

This sale ad for undergarments at Woodward & Lothrop will bring in many customers—just what a sale ad must accomplish.

Semi-Annual

Lycra® spandex* makes the difference when it comes to perfect fitting bras and briefs

Smoother, figure flattering and briefs from your favorite makers. All in Lycra® spandex blends to give you more uplift, control and support.

Pretty Bali® strapless bra
Lace trimmed underwire of nylon-Lycra® spandex. White; sizes 34-38 B,C,D. Reg. 16.50-17.50, **12.37-13.12**

Flower Bali® underwire bra
Embroidered support bra in white or beige nylon-Lycra® spandex. 34-40 B,C, D,DD. Reg. 17.00-19.00, **12.75-14.25**

Bali® Something Else® Briefs of nylon-Lycra® spandex*
Hi-cut leg white, beige, black or moonlight. Sizes S-XL. Reg. 6.50, **sale 4.87**
Tailored white, beige, black, moonlight, blush, M-2X, reg. 6.00, **sale 4.50**
Not shown:
Tummy Control white, beige, black, moonlight, blush, M-2X, reg. 7.50, **sale 5.62**
Cotton Blend white, S-XL, reg. 7.50, **sale 5.62**

*DuPont registered trademark.
**Available at all stores except Fair Oaks, Chevy Chase, Montgomery Mall, Lakeforest, Columbia Mall, Parole Plaza and Pentagon.

Bali® Sno-Flake® firm support underwire bra
White poly-nylon-Lycra® spandex. 34-38 C,D. Reg. 16.50-17.50, **12.37-13.12**

Entire stock of Playtex Limited® bras
Includes all WOW® and Right for Me® styles. Reg. 14.00-19.00, **10.50-14.25**

All Cross Your Heart® bras from Playtex
In white. Reg. 12.50-15.00, **9.38-11.25**
Playtex® racer back Bras
Softcup or underwire. reg. 12.00-14.00, **8.99-10.99**

My Favorite® V-Back® bra by Vanity Fair®
Seamless underwire in white, beige, nylon-Lycra® spandex. 32-36 B,C. Reg. 15.00, **sale 11.25**

WOODWARD & LOTHROP
Woodies is my way

Sale: save 25%

Bras and briefs
from favorite makers
including Warner's,
Olga, Maidenform
and more

A wonderful opportunity to build your
wardrobe with the best of bras and
briefs—and save 25%! The right style
and fit, all in super comfortable Lycra®
spandex blends.

**Warner's® Hidden Powers® softcup
bra** is an all-stretch support style of
nylon-Lycra® spandex. White. Sizes
34-38 B, C,D. Reg. 13.00-14.00,
9.00-10.50

**Warner's® Hidden Powers® comfort
brief** with moderate control and
tummy panel. Nylon-Lycra®
spandex-cotton. White or beige.
M,L,XL,2X. Reg. 18.50,
sale 13.87

**Olga® Bodysilk® contour or padded
bras** in poly-nylon-Lycra® spandex in
white or beige. Sizes 32-36 A,B.
Reg. 15.00-16.50, **11.25-12.37**

**Olga® Wonderwear® light control
brief** in nylon-Lycra® spandex. White
or beige, S,M,L,XL. Reg. 16.00,
sale 12.00

**Warner's® Real McCoy®
contour bra**
Doubleknit nylon tricot with
fiberfill. Nylon Lycra® spandex.
White or beige. 34-36A,B,C.
Reg. 14.00, **sale 10.50**

**Not-all-that-Bra®,
a softcup by Warner's®**
All-stretch seamless support.
Nylon Lycra® spandex.
White or beige. 34-38B,C,D.
Reg. 15.00-16.00, **11.25-12.00**

**Maidenform® Chantilly®
bras and bikinis**
Underwire and softcup bras,
string bikinis.
White, beige, rose.
Reg. 8.00-17.00,
6.00-12.75

**The Pretty Shapely® strapless
by Maidenform®**
Lightly lined, seamless
underwire bra. Poly-nylon
Lycra® spandex in white, beige,
black. 34-36A,B,C.
Reg. 14.50, **sale 10.87**

WOODWARD & LOTHROP

Woodies is my way

The petticoat dress

This page, top to bottom:
Our v-inset blue cotton oxfordcloth, to set afloat
above your favorite petticoat.*
By S.G Gilbert. 4 to 12, 142.00
With a flounce of a hemline. A charming new suit look
in blue cotton chambray over its own attached
eyelet petticoat. By David Warren. 4 to 14, 144.00
With button-tabbed pockets. Wide-belted to make a point of
a tiny waist, in blue-white oxford cotton stripes—
repeated on the hem of its own crinoline petticoat.
By Ronnie Heller for M.J Originals. 4 to 14, 235.00

Opposite page, top to bottom:
With eye-catching embroidery. Our cap-sleeve
dress in soft chambray blue cotton.*
By Depeche. 4 to 12, 132.00
With the slimmest stripes, our exclusive shirtdress
in blue-white cotton by Bonnie Strauss.
4 to 14. 240.00
Wear it over its own eyelet-embroidered petticoat
of fine white cotton. S, M, L, 110.00
With ruffles and ruching. Our droppert-waist
romantic white cotton.*
By S.G Gilbert. 4 to 12, 166.00
Third and Second Floors, Lord & Taylor,
Fifth Avenue at 39th Street
—call (212) 391-1199. Open daily 10 to 6
Thursday 10 to 8. And at Lord & Taylor,
Manhasset, Westchester, Garden City,
Millburn, Ridgewood-Paramus and Stamford
Shop Sundays 12 to 5 at our Manhasset,
Westchester, Garden City, Millburn and
Stamford stores.

The petticoat dress

*The glimpses of petticoat we've added,
our enchantment of hemstitched, flounced,
eyelet-ruffled white cotton. S, M, L, 28.00
just one from a beautiful
new collection on our Fourth Floor

The petticoat dress

Breezy, buoyant, unmistakably
American, with its clean-cut
manners and a cotton crispness
that looks just right now.
The petticoat
that shows beneath
will let you know
that spring is on its way.

The petticoat dress

Lord and Taylor uses a double-page spread to entice its customers with the "petticoat dress." Compare this ad with the Woodward & Lothrop ad on pages 90–91. What can you tell about each stores' customers?

FIVE

THE SEQUENCE

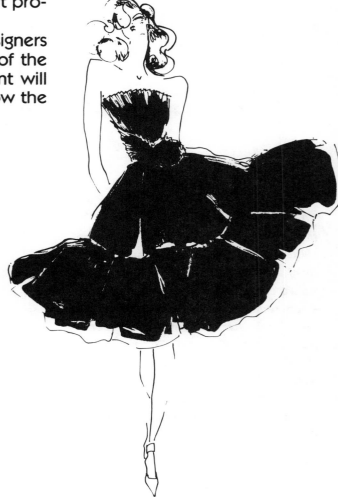

Many different types of fashion art and their function in the fashion industry is illustrated. Together, the pieces form the whole picture. This unit will help clarify the process by showing, in sequence, the design as it progresses through the different stages.

There is no set formula followed by designers and manufacturers. In most cases the size of the firm and the philosophy of the management will determine how the operation is run and how the product is marketed.

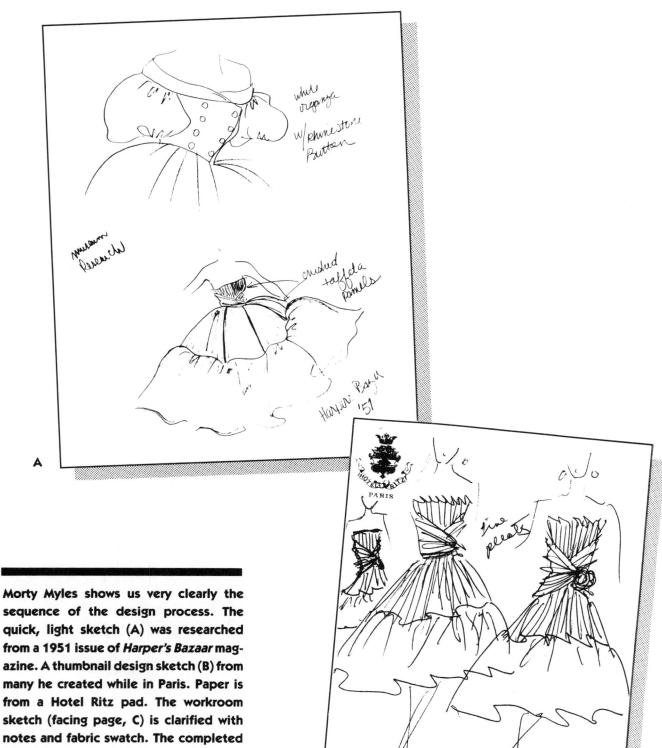

A

B

Morty Myles shows us very clearly the sequence of the design process. The quick, light sketch (A) was researched from a 1951 issue of *Harper's Bazaar* magazine. A thumbnail design sketch (B) from many he created while in Paris. Paper is from a Hotel Ritz pad. The workroom sketch (facing page, C) is clarified with notes and fabric swatch. The completed sketch (D) is in color and could be used as showroom or recordkeeping art by the firm.

C

D

The elements included on these pages are from Jeanne Marc. They include a variety of sketches at each level of the design process and fabric swatches. When planning fabrics and colors, this company will make copies of the design sketches and actually "color" in the garment.

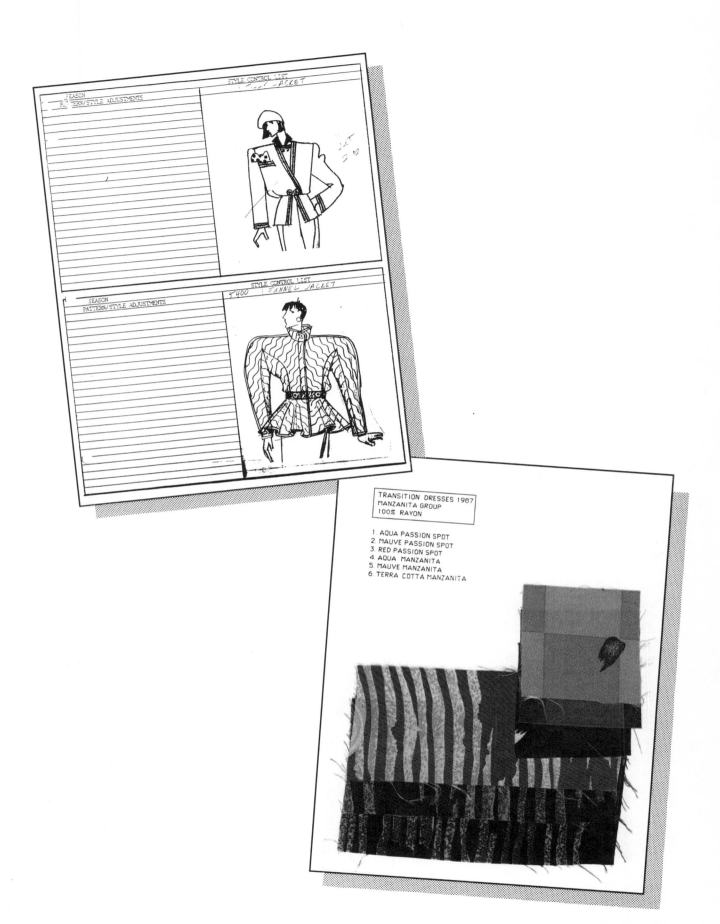

SEASON
PATTERN/STYLE ADJUSTMENTS

STYLE CONTROL LIST
SUIT JACKET

SEASON
PATTERN/STYLE ADJUSTMENTS

STYLE CONTROL LIST
$400   FLANNEL JACKET

TRANSITION DRESSES 1987
MANZANITA GROUP
100% RAYON

1. AQUA PASSION SPOT
2. MAUVE PASSION SPOT
3. RED PASSION SPOT
4. AQUA MANZANITA
5. MAUVE MANZANITA
6. TERRA COTTA MANZANITA

SIX

RELATED AREAS

Many areas are closely related to fashion apparel, but not directly involved in producing and selling apparel. For example, a complete fashion statement or look would not be possible without accessories. This unit will include some examples of art used for the accessories markets as well as cosmetics and fragrances.

Art used in patternbooks, part of the industry devoted to the home sewer is also illustrated here. This industry has grown in sophistication and scope with designer patterns and luxury gift items introduced to an area that once was used primarily as an alternative to purchasing ready-made clothing.

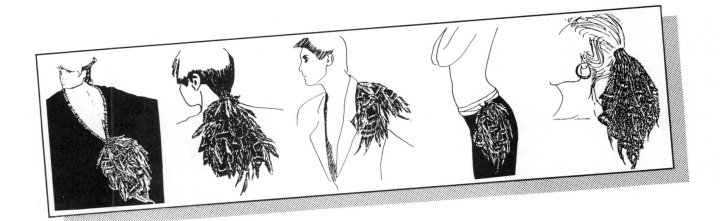

ACCESSORIES

Accessories are to a garment what a frame is to a picture. You can argue the reverse that the garment is the backdrop that sets off the accessory. However, with both arguments there is no doubt that accessories play an important and essential role in fashion. Indeed, dress as we know it from ancient times to the present would not be complete without them. And fashion art can be used to design and merchandise accessories.

What are accessories? Hats, for example, were considered in the past necessary to complete an outfit, but were for some time ignored in fashion. They are now making a strong comeback. Watches are no longer considered just a timepiece, but a fashion accessory.

Watches, jewelry, hats, shoes, hosiery, bags, belts, gloves, scarfs . . . form industries in and of themselves.

Many artists have created reputations and are sought after based on their expertise in these specific areas.

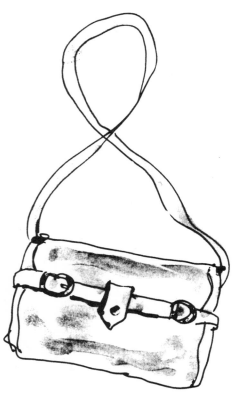

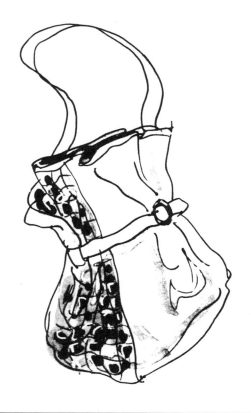

Basic clothing can be changed completely with a select choice of accessories. The fashion head is necessary to show earrings, scarfs, etc. However shoes, belts and handbags can be sketched separately, and without a head or figure.

ACCESSORIES 1

Key areas for development . . .

ESSENTIAL RESEARCH
- French North Africa : the looks and colours.
- Entomological images : scarabs and beetles.
- Inlay techniques and patterning.
- Solid, modern silverwork.
- Wrought iron patternwork.
- Travellers artifacts.

a) Horseshoe shoulder sling. Note woven and leather mixing, concealed front flap fastening.
b) Travelling canvas tote bag. Focus on the folded effect for soft structure, and the stitched, twist over handle.
c) Ruched tote. Linens or canvas pleated or ruched. Leather handles.
d) Pull-on Pirate scarf hat with knotted ends.
e) Knotted crown skullcap with ribbed band.
f) Soft structure silk turban hat.
g) Oversized cuff bracelets. Mixed media concertinas of silver and ebony, or as rippled effect mixed metals.
h) Ivory and coral mixing for triple hoop earrings and amulet bracelet.
i) Facetted and fluid coral twist earrings.

ACCESSORIES 2

a) Focus on the important wider slingback, with the sharply chiselled toe.
b) Transitional walking shoe. Note the bespoke feel Canvas and leather mixing with a tapered stacked heel.
c) Mixed media city court. The bespoke feel contrasts with the sleek high throatline and wider slingback.
d) Multi rouleau sling back sandle. Note the tortoiseshell trim C.F. and longer, block heel.
e) Classic belt update. Tortoiseshell stud fastening and keepers.
f) Soft shaped belt for easy waist emphasis. Rosewood buckle.
g) A chiselled toe and short slightly breasted blocky heel. Use tonal colour or mixed media fabrication.
h) Focus on the new rouleau strap slingback. The tapered, mid height heel is stained black.
i) An elongated mid height stained heel updates the court. Note the cut out side coupled with bespoke detailing.
j) Sling back espadrille as a vehicle for fossil print.

PATTERNBOOKS

Patternbooks are part of an enormous market of products and services available to the home sewer. Sewing machines, sophisticated equipment and a vast selection of fabric sold by the yard are all part of the picture. Class instructions, how-to books, trimmings and notions assist the home sewer to turn out a very professional product.

Fashion sketches are used in patternbooks to sell this product. The sketch is clearly defined as to silhouette and construction details of the garment. The figures used are attractive and, usually, somewhat realistic. A pattern can give a number of variations and the customer can add that personal touch, but the home sewer must relate to the sketch.

Pattern companies supply patterns for women, men, juniors, and children. Special sections are devoted to maternity, bridal and gift items—just to name a few.

There are patterns endorsed by designers and celebrities. Many pattern companies develop a design much the same way as a designer or manufacturer. However, instead of a finished garment, the end result is a pattern that can be used to construct an individualized product.

Art used in promotions by pattern companies has become as upbeat as art in high fashion magazines. This reflects the wide picture of consumer's attraction to "do their own thing." As this attitude changes so has the approach by artists illustrating for this fashion-related industry. The strapless denim dress on the facing page is the original art created for Vogue pattern #9619. You'd be more familiar with it on the pattern cover.

McCall's 2949

Butterick 4643 View C

Butterick 4643 View B

Vogue 1854

Style 4859

Butterick 4636

Simplicity 7920

Burda 6030

Pattern news

Sew skirts that sizzle with the season

S picy bottoms are at the top of the fashion hit parade this season. From suit separates to sporty denim looks, skirts stand out in a myriad of shapes and lengths. Tucks, pleats, godets, yokes and flounces turn simple skirts into spectacular style-builders.

Style 4859 adds pizzazz to a simple straight skirt with a single godet insert in the back center seam. The godet can either be rounded to follow the hemline of the skirt or pointed and elongated to drop below the skirt hem. Either style gives a kick to the rear view.

Butterick 4643 features two versions of a gored trumpet skirt, certainly a fashion staple this season. One view follows the traditional lines of seamed panels from the waistline to the hemline and the other adds a gored flounce to the hemline of a straight skirt. Both sport the sensual lines of fit and flare.

Burda 6030, designed for the denim look that's so popular this season, features a hip yoke, with bold silver zippers at the angled front welt pockets and elongated center front opening. Add jean studs to the yoke and create a black denim skirt that will sizzle with the season!

Issey Miyake adds his asymmetrical flair to **Vogue 1854** for a skirt that certainly depicts the Miyake style. The front yoke is framed with angular seaming on each side, and the hemline is irregular, noticeably longer in front. It's fitted, fun and definitely offers a fashion-forward look.

Pleats are peaking out from all sorts of places, and skirts are a prime target. **McCall's 2949** features a skirt that's partially pleated, front and back. The pleats are stitched down from the waistline to mid-thigh, then flow freely to the hemline to eliminate any extra bulk at the waist and hips. **Butterick 4636** follows the same slimming theory by jazzing up a straight skirt with a rear center panel, accented with knife pleats. **Simplicity 7920** buttons at the waistline and along one side of a center front panel. Once past the hips, the fitted panels become two front and rear box pleats, maintaining the slim silhouette.

So whether you pleat it, gore it, tuck it or flounce it, any one of these skirts will make a statement that spells out fashion '87. ☐

COSMETICS & FRAGRANCES

Makeup changes with the season. New colors and products are continually being introduced. Beauty salons abound. Just think of the changes in hairstyles in recent years. Grooming products and scents for men have also had astounding growth.

In this multi-billion dollar industry, a large percentage of capital is spent on advertising and packaging. Fashion art is used in a special manner in these industries to entice the customer. It takes on a "mood." Full use is made of the fashion head. The environment and the atmosphere surrounding the head as well as the expression are very important.

Many innovative marketing methods are used to reach and convince the consumer that their products are essential. And these messages are conveyed with fashion art!

S E V E N

Y O U R
P O R T F O L I O

A professionally prepared portfolio is essential when applying for a position in the fashion industry. The prospective employer is able to evaluate the skills and knowledge of the applicant, and his/her suitability to their firm.

There is no need nor is it advisable to impress the interviewer with your versatility. Portfolios that include many different types of designs such as bridal gowns, bathing suits and children's wear will lead the interviewer to the conclusion that you are not sure of the area you wish to pursue. A variety of different rendering techniques may also detract from the portfolio.

The interviewer is interested when you show expertise and originality in that company's specialization. So it is a good idea before the interview to gather information relevant to that firm. Go to the retail stores and see the garments they produce. Prepare a portfolio that relates to a generalized category.

An 11″ × 14″ portfolio is the preferred size. It is large enough to present your work and small enough to carry easily. Three or four units will show how you think and your creativity in any given area of design. A unit should consist of a lead page, designs on figures in color, and specs of garment pieces. Plan your pages either vertically or horizontally, but be consistent.

LEAD PAGE

The lead page is very important because it sets the tone and provides the following necessary information:

1. Season and Year
2. Fabric Swatches ... neatly cut (pinked), about 3" × 3", and attached at the top only of the illustration so that they can be touched and felt with one's fingers. (Note the fabric content, e.g., cotton, wool.)
3. A few descriptive words to describe the essence of the line, the color story and what you consider the important pieces and looks.
4. Your name, clearly written.

DESIGNS ON FIGURES IN COLOR

Depending on your design category, you can have two or three figures on a vertical page and three or four figures on a horizontal page. The figure type, face and hairstyle should be appropriate and also enhance the design unit. Add accessories.

SPECS OF GARMENT PIECES

Arrange spec drawings in categories or groups, e.g., blouses, pants, skirts, dresses. Do not work too large. Twelve to eighteen pieces can be shown on two pages.

Note: Back views are shown as they appear on the figure. These can be placed on the page with the design on the figure, if you wish.

A resumé, letter of recommendation or awards should be placed in the inside back cover of the portfolio (in the pocket). Only if your work is acceptable will they be interested in looking at this material. If you feel that your preliminary design concept sketches are good, place them in a clear plastic folder. A designer looking for an assistant is usually pleased to see your thinking process.

Good luck and happy (job) hunting!

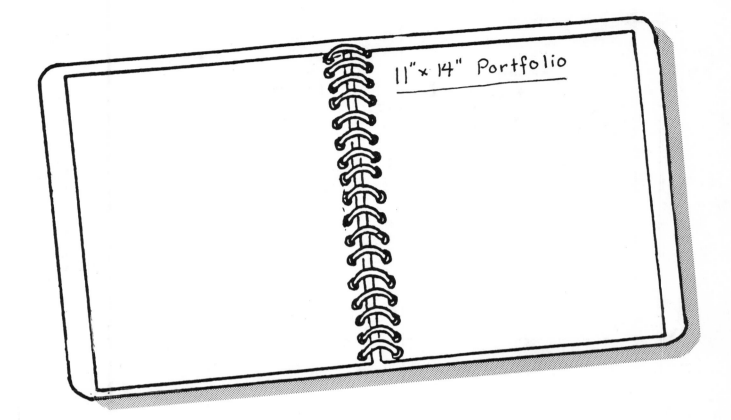

11" x 14" Portfolio

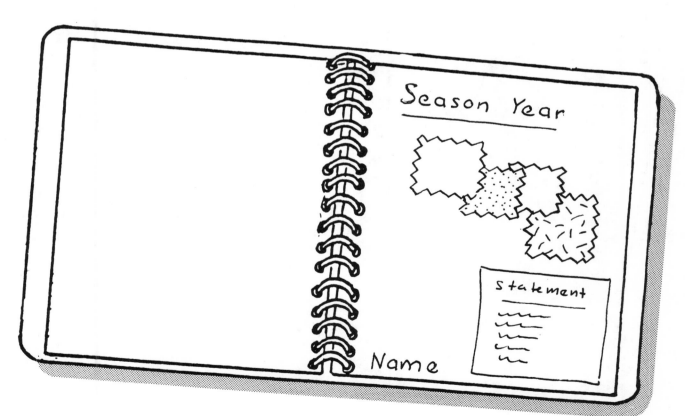

Season Year

statement

Name

**VERTICAL
FORMAT**

HORIZONTAL FORMAT

AND IN CONCLUSION...

Fashion art is all around us. It's found on billboards, on posters, at train platforms or bus stations, on business cards. Think of all the t-shirts imprinted with a stylized form of fashion art. We see gloriously painted fashions in paintings in museums. Fashion figures are used in health and beauty articles for instructional purposes. Theater, opera and dance are highly dependent on fashion design to enhance the mood. And we can always tell the good guys from the bad guys in the movies! I'm sure you can add to this list.

Whether one is strongly involved with fashion, or just puts up with it out of necessity, it is part of our lives and culture. Fashion art is a visual means of communication in one of the largest industries in this world. We all wear clothes, don't we?

ILLUSTRATION CREDITS

American Fabrics & Fashion p. 86
Banana Republic p. 74
Joan Bellew for Joseph Love Inc. p. 19
Bonwit Teller pp. 89, 107
Butterick Company, Inc. pp. 104, 105
Celanese Textile Fibers, Division of Celanese Corporation p. 9
Charles Contreri and Wallace Sloves Ltd. p. 76
Cotton Incorporated p. 9
Louis Dell'Olio and Maurice Antaya, Anne Klein II p. 15, 30, 33,
   40, 41, 69
Diane DeMers p. 27
Ellen Gang for Knitwaves, Inc. p. 29
Walter Gerson p. 37
Harvé Benard Ltd. pp. 47, 65, 82
Here & There p. 5
Carol Horn p. 49
Independent Retailers Syndicate p. 79
Harland Brandon, Italian Trade Commission p. 88
Betsey Johnson p. 14
Michael Kors p. 13
Ron Leal for Betty Hanson & Co. pp. 60, 61, 115
Lord & Taylor pp. 92, 93
Marc Grant for Jeanne Marc pp. 35, 37, 63, 83, 98, 99
Bob Mackie pp. iii, 1, 36, 77, 81
Morton Myles pp. 38, 95, 96, 97
Nigel French Enterprises (U.S.A.) Ltd. pp. 6, 102, 103
Roberta L. Newman p. 101
Doug Rosenthal for Milliken and Company p. 85
Mary Ann Restivo pp. 17, 39, 42−45, 58, 59
George Samen for Lawrence Designs p. 38
Sew News p. 106
George Simantin p. 18
Willi Smith for Williwear pp. 11, 16
Lisa Donofrio for SML Sport Ltd. p. 48
Monika Tilley p. 19
Tobé Associates Inc. p. 7
Joseph Vincent p. 62
Woodward & Lothrop pp. 90, 91
WWD p. 85